D1554875

DIONYSOS

Dionysos is our oldest living symbol. First mentioned in texts of the thirteenth century BC, he was for the ancient Greeks the divine embodiment of wine, of mystery-cult, and of the theatre, and even today is valued as a symbol of something fundamental to being human. With the power of his epiphany Dionysos broke down the barriers of individual consciousness, he merged the individual into the group. He did it not only by wine, but also in the transformation of individuals in the theatre, and in the rehearsal of death in mystery-cult. In this way Dionysos could embody the whole community, but could also be a refined philosophical symbol.

He was the most serious rival to the spread of Christianity, by which he was not entirely eliminated: his resurgences in Renaissance Italy and nineteenth-century Germany are described in the final chapter of this book. *Dionysos*, a groundbreaking survey of one of the most enduring of Greek gods, provides an excellent reference point for study and will also be of interest to readers in related disciplines.

Richard Seaford is a Professor in the Department of Classics at Exeter. His books include commentaries on the two Dionysiac plays of Euripides and *Reciprocity and Ritual: Homer and Tragedy in the Developing City-State.*

Gods and Heroes of the Ancient World

Series editor Susan Deacy
Roehampton University

Routledge is pleased to present an exciting new series, Gods and Heroes of the Ancient World. These figures from antiquity are embedded in our culture, many functioning as the source of creative inspiration for poets, novelists, artists, composers and filmmakers. Concerned with their multifaceted aspects within the world of ancient paganism and how and why these figures continue to fascinate, the books provide a route into understanding Greek and Roman polytheism in the 21st century.

These concise and comprehensive guides provide a thorough understanding of each figure, offering the latest in critical research from the leading scholars in the field in an accessible and approachable form, making them ideal for undergraduates in Classics and related disciplines.

Each volume includes illustrations, time charts, family trees and maps where appropriate.

Also available:

Zeus
Keith Dowden

Prometheus
Carol Dougherty

Medea
Emma Griffiths

Susan Deacy is Lecturer in Greek History and Literature at Roehampton University. Her main research interests are Greek religion, and gender and sexuality. Publications include the co-edited volumes *Rape in Antiquity* (1997) and *Athena in the Classical World* (2001), and the monograph *A Traitor to Her Sex? Athena the Trickster* (forthcoming).

DIONYSOS

Richard Seaford

LONDON AND NEW YORK

First published 2006
by Routledge
2 Park Square, Milton Park, Abingdon, Oxon OX14 4RN

Simultaneously published in the USA and Canada
by Routledge
270 Madison Avenue, New York, NY 10016

*Routledge is an imprint of the Taylor & Francis Group,
an informa business*

Designed and typeset in Utopia by
Keystroke, Jacaranda Lodge, Wolverhampton
Printed and bound in Great Britain by
TJ International Ltd, Padstow, Cornwall

British Library Cataloguing in Publication Data
A catalogue record for this book is available from the British Library

Library of Congress Cataloging in Publication Data
Seaford, Richard.
    Dionysos / Richard Seaford.
        p. cm.
    Includes bibliographical references and index.
    ISBN 0–415–32488–2 (pbk. : alk. paper) — ISBN 0–415–32487–4
    (hardback : alk. paper)
    1. Dionysus (Greek deity) I. Title.
    BL820.B2S43 2006
    292.2′113—dc22   2006003271

ISBN 10: 0–415–32487–4 (hbk)
ISBN 10: 0–415–32488–2 (pbk)
ISBN 10: 0–203–35801–5 (ebk)
ISBN 13: 978–0–415–32487–8 (hbk)
ISBN 13: 978–0–415–32488–5 (pbk)
ISBN 13: 978–0–203–35801–6 (ebk)

CONTENTS

SERIES FOREWORD

For a person who is about to embark on any serious discourse or task, it is proper to begin first with the gods.

(Demosthenes, *Letters* 1.1)

WHY GODS AND HEROES?

The gods and heroes of classical antiquity are part of our culture. Many function as sources of creative inspiration for poets, novelists, artists, composers, filmmakers and designers. Greek tragedy's enduring appeal has ensured an ongoing familiarity with its protagonists' experiences and sufferings, while the choice of Minerva as the logo of one of the newest British universities, the University of Lincoln, demonstrates the ancient gods' continued emblematic potential. Even the world of management has used them as representatives of different styles: Zeus and the 'club' culture for example, and Apollo and the 'role' culture: see C. Handy, *The Gods of Management: who they are, how they work and why they fail* (London, 1978).

This series is concerned with how and why these figures continue to fascinate and intrigue. But it has another aim too, namely to explore their strangeness. The familiarity of the gods and heroes risks obscuring a vital difference between modern meanings and ancient functions and purpose. With certain exceptions, people today do not worship them, yet to the Greeks and Romans they were real beings in a system comprising literally hundreds of divine powers. These range from the major gods, each of whom was worshipped in many guises via their epithets or 'surnames', to the heroes – deceased individuals associated with local communities – to other figures such as daimons and nymphs. The landscape was dotted with sanctuaries, while natural features such as mountains, trees and rivers were thought to be inhabited by religious beings. Studying ancient paganism involves finding strategies to comprehend a world where everything was, in the often quoted words of Thales, 'full of gods'.

In order to get to grips with this world, it is necessary to set aside our preconceptions of the divine, shaped as they are in large part by Christianised notions of a transcendent, omnipotent God who is morally good. The Greeks and Romans worshipped numerous beings, both male and female, who looked, behaved and suffered like humans, but who, as immortals, were not bound by the human condition. Far from being omnipotent, each had limited powers: even the sovereign, Zeus/Jupiter, shared control of the universe with his brothers Poseidon/Neptune (the sea) and Hades/Pluto (the underworld). Lacking a creed or anything like an organised church, ancient paganism was open to continual reinterpretation, with the result that we should not expect to find figures with a uniform essence. It is common to begin accounts of the pantheon with a list of the major gods and their function(s) (Hephaistos/Vulcan: craft; Aphrodite/Venus: love; and Artemis/Diana: the hunt and so on), but few are this straightforward. Aphrodite, for example, is much more than the goddess of love, vital though that function is. Her epithets include *Hetaira* ('courtesan') and *Porne* ('prostitute'), but also attest roles as varied as patron of the citizen body (*Pandemos*: 'of all the people') and protectress of seafaring (*Euploia, Pontia, Limenia*).

Recognising this diversity, the series consists not of biographies of each god or hero (though such have been attempted in the past), but of investigations into their multifaceted aspects within the complex world of ancient paganism. Its approach has been shaped partly in response to two distinctive patterns in previous research. Until the middle of the twentieth century, scholarship largely took the form of studies of individual gods and heroes. Many works presented a detailed appraisal of such issues as each figure's origins, myth and cult; these include L.R. Farnell's examination of major deities in his *Cults of the Greek States* (5 vols, Oxford, 1896–1909) and A.B. Cook's huge three-volume *Zeus* (Cambridge, 1914–40). Others applied theoretical developments to the study of gods and heroes, notably (and in the closest existing works to a uniform series) K. Kerényi in his investigations of gods as Jungian archetypes, including *Prometheus: archetypal image of human existence* (English trans. London 1963) and *Dionysos: archetypal image of the indestructable life* (English trans. London 1976).

In contrast, under the influence of French structuralism, the later part of the century saw a deliberate shift away from research into particular gods and heroes towards an investigation of the system of which they were part. Fuelled by a conviction that the study of isolated gods could not do justice to the dynamics of ancient religion, the pantheon came to be represented as a logical and coherent network in which the various powers were systematically opposed to one another. In a classic study by J.-P. Vernant, for example, the Greek concept of space was shown to be consecrated through the opposition between Hestia (goddess of the hearth – fixed space) and Hermes (messenger and traveller god – moveable space: Vernant, *Myth and Thought Among the Greeks*, London, 1983, 127–75). The gods as individual entities were far from neglected however, as may be exemplified by the works by Vernant, and his colleague M. Detienne, on particular deities including Artemis, Dionysos and Apollo: see, most recently, Detienne's *Apollon, le couteau en main: une approche expérimentale du polythéisme grec* (Paris, 1998).

In a sense, this series is seeking a middle ground. While approaching its subjects as unique (if diverse) individuals, it pays attention to their significance as powers within the collectivity of religious beings. *Gods and Heroes of the Ancient World* sheds new light on many of the most important religious beings of classical antiquity; it also provides a route into understanding Greek and Roman polytheism in the twenty-first century.

The series is intended to interest the general reader as well as being geared to the needs of students in a wide range of fields from Greek and Roman religion and mythology, classical literature and anthropology, to Renaissance literature and cultural studies. Each book presents an authoritative, accessible and refreshing account of its subject via three main sections. The introduction brings out what it is about the god or hero that merits particular attention. This is followed by a central section which introduces key themes and ideas, including (to varying degrees) origins, myth, cult and representations in literature and art. Recognising that the heritage of myth is a crucial factor in its continued appeal, the reception of each figure since antiquity forms the subject of the third part of the book. The volumes include illustrations of each god/hero and where appropriate time charts, family trees and maps. An annotated bibliography synthesises past research and indicates useful follow-up reading.

For convenience, the masculine terms 'gods' and 'heroes' have been selected for the series title, although (and with an apology for the male-dominated language), the choice partly reflects ancient usage in that the Greek *theos* ('god') is used of goddesses too. For convenience and consistency, Greek spellings are used for ancient names, except for famous Latinised exceptions, and BC/AD has been selected rather than BCE/CE.

I am indebted to Catherine Bousfield, the editorial assistant until 2004, who (literally) dreamt up the series and whose thoroughness and motivation brought it close to its launch. The hard work and efficiency of her successor, Matthew Gibbons, has overseen its progress to publication, and the classics editor of Routledge, Richard Stoneman, has provided support and expertise throughout. The anonymous readers for each proposal gave frank and helpful advice, while the authors' commitment to advancing scholarship while producing accessible accounts of their designated subjects has made it a pleasure to work with them.

Susan Deacy, Roehampton University, June 2005

ILLUSTRATIONS

WHY DIONYSOS?

INTRODUCING DIONYSOS

INTRODUCTION: THE UNITY OF DIONYSOS

The name of the god Dionysos first appears on a clay tablet from the Greek bronze age, over three thousand years ago. And so he is our oldest living symbol.

A symbol of what? He does not, in his various manifestations, symbolise the same thing. Plutarch (1st to 2nd centuries AD) noted that he is represented in many forms (*Moralia* 389b). It is the same with other deities. What does the Olympian Zeus share, apart from the name, with the Zeus who was represented as a snake? Does the meaning of Jesus Christ for, say, George W. Bush have anything at all in common with his meaning for, say, Francis of Assisi?

The various processes and experiences associated with Dionysos may seem to us to have no connection with each other. And yet many of them (though not all) do in fact form a unity. This may seem surprising to anyone who looks down the chapter headings of this book. What, for instance, does epiphany have to do with theatre, or 'communality' with death? The way in which we divide up our experience is unable to make such connections. But our divisions are specific to our own time and place. Other cultures, including the ancient Greek, divide things up differently. In fact the chapter headings – as will become clear – refer to aspects of the same entity, and to realise this is to broaden our experience of the world.

WHY DOES DIONYSOS MATTER
IN THE MODERN WORLD?

Why, in the twenty-first century, should anybody be interested in the ancient Greek god Dionysos? From the Internet alone we can make the acquaintance of a hundred living religions, whereas the cult of Dionysos, and the ecstasy he inspired, died long ago.

But the passing away of Dionysos raises a doubt. The psychological fragmentation and manipulated homogeneity of our media-dominated consumerism may create an intense need for some kind of transcendence. It is a need that, for most people, cannot be fulfilled by institutionalised religion, in part because such religion is inextricably wedded to forms of social control that tend to limit the moral and religious experience of the controlled. Nor can it be fulfilled by the cheap forms of spiritual liberation on offer from various religious cults.

True liberation from the consumerist mind-set can be achieved only by finding a perspective from which to perceive its narrowness. And in the search for this perspective enormous resources may be found in the past, albeit not in the fragmented past purveyed to the modern consumer: true liberation always requires mental focus.

I am not of course suggesting that we should revive the cult of Dionysos. Rather, Dionysos provides a perspective on the narrowness of modern religious experience, and helps us to understand how different kinds of society tend to produce different forms of religious organisation and experience. There are various reasons why Dionysos is more helpful than are other alien gods in providing these perspectives on our own insularity.

First, when Christianity was establishing itself in the ancient Mediterranean world, the cult of Dionysos was its most geographically widespread and deeply rooted rival. And so the Christian church, while enclosing the revolutionary ethics of its gospels within the necessity of social control, was influenced by Dionysiac cult as well as opposing it.

Second, until the triumph of Christianity the cult of Dionysos had flourished throughout the recorded history of the Greeks, for a thousand years, always having at its heart the power of Dionysos to bridge the gaps between the three spheres of the world – nature, humanity, and divinity. Humanity emerges from nature and aspires to divinity. Dionysos, by transcending these fundamental divisions, may *transform the identity* of an individual into animal and god. And it is by his presence that he liberates the individual from the circumstances of this life. In these respects Dionysos contrasts with the relatively remote and austere god of Christianity. A small but telling symptom of the contrast is the early and persistent Christian hostility to the *mask*, as diabolical. It is the joyful transformation of identity that underlies the importance of Dionysos in various spheres – notably the spheres of wine, mystery-cult, the underworld, politics, theatre, poetry, philosophy, and visual art.

And indeed Dionysos – more than any other ancient Greek deity – fills a modern need. He remains a symbol of something important that cannot be so effectively expressed in any other way. For instance, Richard Schechner, who directed the seminal New York performance of *Dionysus in 69*, wrote in an essay entitled *The Politics of Ecstasy* (1968) that Dionysos 'is present in today's America – showing himself in the hippies, in the "carnival spirit" of black insurrectionists, on campuses; and even, in disguise, on the patios and in the living rooms of suburbia'. In the same tradition, *The God of Ecstasy: Sex-Roles and the Madness of Dionysos* by Arthur Evans (1988) is a sustained invocation of Dionysos as embodying the forces required to save our civilisation from militarism, individualism, unfeeling intellect, greedy destruction of the natural environment, male-dominated hierarchy, and the conversion of people into objects. The book culminates in an account of the 'affirmation of the whole self through ecstatic ritual' in a homosexual ritual orgy on a California beach.

It is not only in the outlandish practices of the American counter-culture that Dionysos has survived, but even – under the influence of Friedrich Nietzsche (1844–1900) – in the elaborate abstractions of contemporary European philosophy, as we shall see at the end of Chapter 10.

There is of course an enormous difference between the ancient and the modern Dionysos. For the ancient Greeks Dionysos was believed to be a god, and was given cult. But in our very different world, and notably since Nietzsche's *Birth of Tragedy* (1872), he seems rather to be a symbol of a certain mental state – or at most the name for whatever it is that produces that mental state. Dionysos has become the Dionysiac. And yet it is not impossible that the mental state that required and produced the ancient belief in Dionysos as a god overlaps with the modern mental state that keeps alive the Dionysiac as an irreducible symbol.

PREVIOUS VERSIONS OF DIONYSOS

Readers anxious to meet the god himself may want to omit this section. But the reason for introducing here a survey of earlier accounts of the god is that they inevitably influence the categories that we choose in approaching him today. Moreover, however much they differ from each other and from this book, these accounts are all strangely compelling. No book on Dionysos can be definitive.

The modern study of Dionysos begins with Nietzsche's *The Birth of Tragedy*, in which there are four features of the Dionysiac that have set the agenda for much subsequent writing. First, Nietzsche privileges – as especially Dionysiac – Athenian *tragedy*. Whether he is right to do so depends on the problem, that is still debated among scholars, of whether the content of Athenian tragedy can be said to be Dionysiac (see Chapter 7).

Second, Nietzsche emphasises *contradiction*. In antiquity Dionysos is occasionally described in ways that suggest his duality or embodiment of opposites. Nietzsche makes this a more sublime and central feature: 'in Dionysiac conditions . . . the contradiction (*Widerspruch*), the joy born of pain, declared itself from the heart of nature' (§4). The Dionysiac artist is 'entirely united with the primal unity (*Ur-Eine*), its pain and contradiction' (§5).

The idea of experiencing a primal *unity* brings me to the third feature, Nietzsche's emphasis on the *dissolution of boundaries* – notably between man and man, and between man and nature.

Fourth, Nietzsche abstracts the Dionysiac from history and makes it into a *metaphysical* principle. For instance, he describes the synthesis of the Dionysiac (ecstatic disorder) and the Apolline (individuated order) in the genesis of tragedy as arising from 'a metaphysical miracle of the Hellenic will' (§1). I will return to Nietzsche in Chapter 10.

The Birth of Tragedy has, since its first appearance, been rejected by most professional Hellenists for its poor scholarship. But it was initially championed by Nietzsche's friend Erwin Rohde (1845–98). Subsequently, in his *Psyche* (1894), Rohde provided a much more scholarly version of Nietzsche's focus on the ecstatic *experience* of the Dionysiac. Whereas Nietzsche writes lyrically of the transformative effect of the Dionysiac, in which man 'feels himself as a god', Rohde catalogues the *empirical evidence* for the various forms of Dionysiac exaltation of the soul (including the identification of man with god).

Rohde focuses on ideas of the soul after death, and this introduces a whole dimension of the Dionysiac that is missing from Nietzsche. His interest is not in the metaphysics but in the practicalities of the ecstasy, and in the historical development of the cult. And whereas for Nietzsche Dionysos is thoroughly Greek, Rohde believed (wrongly: see Chapter 2) that he originated in Thrace. For Nietzsche the synthesis of the Dionysiac with the Apolline is metaphysical, but for Rohde it is, if anything, a historical event – the incorporation of Thracian ecstatic cult into the more austere religion of the Greeks.

Rohde's combination of broad outlook with mastery of detail has had considerable influence, notably on E. R. Dodds (1893–1979), who in his commentary on Euripides' *Bacchae* (first edition 1944) adapted the inheritance of Rohde to Freudian psychology, maintaining that 'to resist Dionysus is to repress the elemental in one's own nature'.

Nine years after Rohde's *Psyche* Jane Harrison (1850–1928) published her *Prolegomena to the Study of Greek Religion*. The chapter on Dionysos focuses on his associations with nature (notably the vine and the bull), within the evolutionary scheme – pioneered by the comparative anthropologist J. G. Frazer – of the prehistoric development of primitive magic into religion. Her proclaimed aim is to establish the detailed study of *ritual*, rather than myth or literature, as the 'first preliminary' to understanding Greek religion.

In Harrison's subsequent *Themis* (1912) her account of Greek religion remains developmental, but Dionysos has acquired special significance as the only deity to be constantly accompanied by a thiasos (sacred band or retinue). Influenced by Durkheim (1858–1917), she has come to understand Dionysos as – unlike the 'Olympians' – arising out of the emotions and desires of the *group*. Accordingly she admires Nietzsche's association of Dionysos with the dissolution of boundaries, but for her the essence of Dionysos is to be seen not as metaphysical (Nietzsche) or spiritual (Rohde) but as *social*.

Of the various accounts of Dionysos in the first half of the twentieth century there are two that, in relation to Nietzsche, represent opposite extremes. Walter Otto (1987–1958), taking further Nietzsche's focus on contradiction, produces an ahistorical vision of a thoroughly Greek Dionysos who is distinguished from the Olympians by the 'spirit of duality', especially the duality of life and death (*Dionysos. Myth and Cult*, German original 1933).

At the opposite pole are the painstaking, empirical reconstructions of the historical development of Dionysiac cults by Martin Nilsson (1874–1967). For Nilsson the cult of Dionysos is *practical*, concerned mainly with the promotion of fertility. In sharp contrast to Nietzsche, Nilsson's Dionysos is in the Frazerian tradition, part of a historical development or evolution, a phase in our struggle to master the environment, and of Asian origin. It has no place for such Nietzschean abstractions as contradiction, the dissolution of boundaries, or primal unity.

But in the second half of the twentieth century the battle lines were not so clearly drawn: conceptions of Dionysos tended, as earlier those of Rohde and Harrison, to combine concrete details of cult and myth with Nietzschean abstractions.

A concept that is crucial for understanding Dionysos, and much of what has been written about him, is *contradiction*. For Nietzsche contradiction (*Widerspruch*) belongs to the primal unity, but 'eternal contradiction' is called 'the father of things'. But how can the same (primal, eternal) thing have both unity and contradiction? Only if two opposites both (a) combine to form a unity, and yet (b) somehow retain their identity as opposites. But between (a) and (b) there is in fact a spectrum, along which Nietzsche's mysterious conception seems to oscillate.

Karl Kerényi (1897–1973) derived Dionysos from Minoan Crete, and – like Nietzsche – associated Dionysos with the idea of the indestructibility of life. But for Kerényi the idea has become an archetype of the kind popularised by Carl Jung (1875–1961), and (in contrast to Nietzsche) the opposites of life and death are definitely integrated into a unity – indestructible life. In Dionysiac festivals 'the paradoxical union of life and death, dominated by life, is realized' (200). Accordingly, Otto's association of Dionysos with life that 'is intimately associated with death' is modified by Kerényi (132) into indestructible life that 'is tested (though not affected in its inmost core) by its diametric opposite, *thanatos*' (death). On the Nietzschean spectrum, Otto's conception is at the pole of unreconciled duality (b), whereas Kerényi's tends to integrated unity (a).

'The primary effect of Dionysiac tragedy', according to Nietzsche, 'is this, that the state and society, and generally the gulfs between man and man, yield to an overwhelming feeling of unity that leads back to the heart of nature' (§7). This opposition, between 'the state and society' on the one hand and the Dionysiac dissolution of boundaries on the other, reappears in Marcel Detienne's *Dionysos Slain* (French original 1977). He states that the Dionysiac *ōmophagy* – the eating raw of a hunted animal by people possessed by Dionysos – 'annihilated the barriers erected by the politico-religious system between gods, beasts, and men' (88). 'Dionysiac religion' is an 'anti-system' (59) and 'protest movement' (62), which 'contests the official religion' (64).

For Nietzsche the result of this dissolution of boundaries is a feeling of *unity* (at the heart of nature), whereas for Detienne it is for the sake of another *opposition* – between the Dionysiac mode of killing and eating animals and that of the city-state (polis). In the structuralist theory of myth a concrete opposition tends to embody a more abstract one: in the application of this theory by Detienne the opposition between raw and cooked meat embodies the opposition between Dionysiac and official religion.

In fact *ōmophagy* was – so far as we know – almost entirely confined to *myth*. If ever practised in ritual, it probably lacked the savagery that it symbolised. In the abstraction of his account Detienne tends, on our Nietzschean spectrum, to the pole of unreconciled duality of opposites (b). But the symbolic expression in ritual of contradiction between savagery and civilisation may in reality have been a means of political *integration* (a). Detienne's account has the advantage of including the polis, but his idea of the polis is abstract and timeless: it ignores the enormous importance of Dionysiac cults in the religious calendar of the polis, and excludes historical development.

A similar position on our spectrum is occupied by Detienne's Parisian colleague Jean-Paul Vernant, who has combined it with two influential developments in the idea of Dionysiac contradiction. One is to identify Dionysos not just with the co-existence of opposites but also – by a shift of perspective to within the opposition – with the *unfamiliar* or *disruptive* opposite, the sudden intrusion of *otherness* or 'the other' (for instance the barbarian for a Greek, the female for a male). Second, the range of this 'otherness' becomes universal. Dionysos 'transcends *all* forms and evades *all* definitions; he assumes *all* aspects without confining himself to any one' (emphases added). He calls the human and social order 'into question'.

It is in accordance with this remarkable range of interrogative activity ('calling into question') that for Charles Segal in his book on Euripides' *Bacchae* (1982) 'Dionysos operates as the principle that destroys differences', even 'the difference between symbol and referent', with the result that 'our very construction of reality through perception, thought and language is called into question' (234–5).

Finally, the universalism of Vernant is combined with the unintegrated duality of Otto by Oudemans and Lardinois in their *Tragic Ambiguity* (1987). While recognising that Dionysos may embody order, they nevertheless insist that 'for Dionysiac logic there is no harmony and no solving of contradictions in any phase of development. It reveals the co-existence of order and disorder' (216).

Lacking immunity to intellectual fashion, these highly abstract conceptions of the 1980s make Dionysos into the god of antistructure *in general*, including even the semantic instability that fascinates the postmodern academy. Moreover, opposites are not just unreconciled but irreconcilable. This takes us beyond pole (b) on our Nietzschean spectrum.

I have selected for discussion some of the overall conceptions of the Dionysiac since Nietzsche, without mentioning the enormous amount of vital work that has been done on collecting and interpreting the evidence of different kinds. Recent work of this kind includes the studies of Dionysos in drama by Bierl and by Lada-Richards, the contrasting treatments of the early vase-painting by Carpenter and

Isler-Kerényi, the detailed examination of local cults by Casadio, the incisive series of papers by Henrichs, the close examination of Dionysiac texts by Schlesier, and the collection of Dionysiac inscriptions by Jaccottet and of Dionysiac sarcophagi by Matz. Indebted though I am to work of this kind, my task is the different one of providing yet another overall account of this perennially fascinating god. Although introductory, it is not without new ideas. And it is enriched by work (including archaeological discoveries) unavailable to the authors of previous such accounts, and informed by my view of their successes and failures.

One failure, it seems to me, is the over-abstractness, from Nietzsche onwards, of metaphysical conceptions of Dionysos that have the appeal of facilitating the schematic organisation of some of the vast mass of Dionysiac material. Some of these conceptions are strikingly at odds with each other, in part because they focus on different material. My aim is to produce not only a representative sample of the enormous amount of evidence for Dionysos in Graeco-Roman antiquity but also an overall conception of Dionysos that – by being always grounded in ancient practice and belief – will bring out the coherence of much of it, but without ignoring what the conception cannot illuminate.

It will for instance be clear from Chapters 5 and 8 that the 'Dionysiac' ideas of the unity of opposites and the dissolution of boundaries are comprehensible only if envisaged as *pragmatic*, as grounded in the reality of mystery-cult and its concomitant beliefs. This grounding exposes the association of Dionysos with unreconciled or irreconcilable opposites, or with a generalised 'otherness', as misleading abstractions.

My overall conception arises from the power of Dionysos to *transform individual identity*. The primary context for such transformation is mystery-cult, which accordingly is the theme of my longest chapter (5). It is from this perspective, I believe, that the material acquires most coherence. The Dionysiac dissolution of the boundaries of individual identity pervades the whole book.

OVERVIEW

Dionysos exists in our own world, as an irreducible symbol for the antithesis of something basically wrong with our society. When we look at modern conceptions of Dionysos since Friedrich Nietzsche, we frequently find a Dionysos who embodies something that is beneath the surface of our society and somehow embodies a universal challenge to it. Are such conceptions mere abstractions, remote from the reality of the ancient Dionysos? To some extent they are, and yet not entirely – as we shall see in what follows.

KEY THEMES

2

NATURE

INTRODUCTION

For many centuries of European history Dionysos was thought of as the god of wine, or of the unrestrained joys of nature (as for instance in the Titian painting reproduced as Figure 7). But the unrestrained joys of nature are an urban vision. For most people in ancient societies life was a struggle to *control* nature. And so it was important to win the favour of what we call the powers of nature, what they imagined as deities. Prominent among such deities was Dionysos. To be sure, given his pervasive power, his activity was not confined to the vineyard. But just as the production of food is a precondition for all other human activities, so there is a sense in which Dionysos' association with 'nature' is basic to the various activities to be described in this book, and so that is where we start.

WINE

In the thirteenth century BC economic records were written in Greek on tablets in a script known as Linear B. On three of these tablets, from Pylos in the western Peloponnese and from Chania in Crete, the name Dionysos appears for the first time, in the Chania tablet along with the name of Zeus. Although it has been argued that one of the Pylos tablets also provides evidence for Dionysos' connection with wine, this is uncertain. But given that Greek viticulture was already important in this period, and that it was certainly associated with Dionysos from the seventh century BC throughout Graeco-Roman antiquity, it is likely that this association stretched back also into the relatively unknown centuries from the thirteenth to the seventh BC. Our first certain evidence of the association is in the oldest surviving Greek poetry. Dionysos is mentioned briefly in Homeric epic four times, of which two imply an association with wine: at *Iliad* 14.325 he is called a 'joy for mortals', and at Odyssey 24.74–6 he is the donor to Thetis of the golden amphora that is eventually to contain the bones of her son Achilles in unmixed wine and oil. The amphora was generally used for wine (e.g. *Odyssey* 2.290), as well as having here the association with death characteristic of Dionysos (Chapter 6). It is difficult to date these references: much of Homeric epic derives from the eighth century BC, but it probably did not take its final form before the sixth. Hesiod, who seems to have lived around 700 BC, speaks of wine as 'gifts of Dionysos' (*Works and Days* 614). The poet Archilochus, who was active in the middle of the seventh century BC, claims to know how to sing – with his mind 'thunderbolted with wine' – the song of Dionysos, the dithyramb (fragment 120).

In the sixth and fifth centuries the most abundant evidence for Dionysos as the god of wine is in Athenian vase-painting. Many of the vases were used to contain wine, and are accordingly often decorated with pictures of Dionysos and of his retinue of 'silens' or 'satyrs' – hedonistic males with some equine characteristics, fond of revelry, sex, music, and wine. The god frequently carries a drinking vessel, the satyrs are often engaged in the production (picking and treading grapes) and the transport of wine, sometimes in the presence of Dionysos, and the scenes are often decorated with vines.

Of special interest is one of the very earliest (c. 570 BC) surviving pictures of Dionysos, by Sophilos (Figure 1) in his vase-painting of the wedding of Peleus and Thetis: Dionysos walks in a procession of deities towards the bridegroom Peleus, who is standing in front of his house, facing the procession, and holding a *kantharos* (drinking cup). Dionysos holds up in front of him a grape-vine, presumably as a gift for Peleus. A little later the same scene was painted by Kleitias (on the 'François Vase' in Florence): Dionysos again carries a grape-vine, but also carries on his shoulder an amphora (no doubt in this context a

Figure 1 Attic dinos painted by Sophilos.

Source: © Courtesy of the Trustees of the British Museum.

wine-jar), and – despite moving rightwards in the procession – his mask-like face is turned to stare straight at the viewer.

On both vases Dionysos seems less civilised or more rustic than the other deities in the procession. In Sophilos' painting he is barefoot and walking rather than in a chariot, in Kleitias' he is barefoot and long-bearded. And whereas what he carries, the grape-vine, is taken directly from nature, the wine-cup carried by Peleus contains the grape-vine transformed by culture.

The festival called Anthesteria was celebrated in honour of Dionysos by many Ionian communities, although the details of its enactment are known almost entirely from Athens. Celebrated in late February, it centred on the opening and drinking of the wine produced in the previous autumn. In the autumn, at the time of the vintage and wine-pressing, the Athenians celebrated the Oschophoria, named after the bunches of grapes on branches carried in procession. The vintage was an event of joyful and seasonally determined communality as well as of economic significance, and the evidence for it being accompanied by Dionysiac celebration is found throughout antiquity. In the pastoral romance *Daphnis and Chloe* by Longus (c. AD 200), erotic desire at a vintage festival on Lesbos is said to be appropriate to 'a festival of Dionysos and the birth of wine' (2.2.1). The association of the vintage with Dionysos lasted – to judge by Christian condemnation (Chapter 9) – into the late seventh century AD.

THE ANTHESTERIA

I mention briefly here various aspects of the Anthesteria that are characteristic of Dionysiac cult generally, and will return to each of them in a subsequent chapter.

First, not even slaves or children were excluded from the wine-drinking. Wine is communally celebrated not only because its production is communal but also because its transformative effect may, in being enjoyed by all male members of the community, tend to remove barriers between them. It was Dionysos, according to the chorus of Euripides' *Bacchae* (421–3), who 'gave the pain-removing delight of wine equally to the wealthy man and to the lesser man'. Though in the paintings by Sophilos and Kleitias Dionysos seems less aristocratic than the other gods, the wine he brings is needed for the aristocratic wedding-feast. We will see that it was wine, administered by Dionysos, that reintegrated the artisan Hephaistos into the community of Olympian gods. In *Daphnis and Chloe* the owners of the country estate leave their town dwellings to join the rural workers in celebrating the vintage. To the communality inspired by Dionysos I will return in Chapter 3.

Second, at the Anthesteria it seems that Dionysos was escorted into the city in a cart shaped like a ship in a procession (depicted in vase-paintings). In the *Homeric Hymn* to Dionysos the god takes the form of a young man, is captured by pirates, and makes his epiphany (as a lion) on their ship, accompanied by miracles that include a spring of wine, the appearance of a vine with abundant grape-bunches along the top of the sail, and the transformation of the pirates into dolphins. A wonderful sixth-century BC vase-painting by Exekias depicts the scene (Figure 2). In the paintings of Dionysos in the ship-cart procession he is holding up a vine that stretches the length of the ship: this suggests that the procession commemorated the mythical epiphany. The arrival of Dionysos to public acclamation is also an *epiphany* (Chapter 4).

It was imagined that, perhaps at the conclusion of the procession, Dionysos was sexually united with the wife of the 'king' (in fact a magistrate) in the old royal house. This resembles the myth of Dionysos arriving at the house of Oeneus (king of Calydon in Aetolia) and having sex with his wife. Oeneus, whose name means 'wine man', tactfully withdrew, and was rewarded with the gift of the vine. This symbolic limitation on the autonomy of the royal household benefits – as does the opening of the new wine – the community as a whole.

Figure 2 Attic kylix painted by Exekias.

Dionysos may make his epiphany at his festival not only by entering the city but also as a miraculous spring of wine, with which he may be identified (Chapter 5). According to Pausanias (second century AD) the people of Elis assert that Dionysos comes to their festival: three pots are placed empty inside a temple of Dionysos, the doors are sealed, and the next day the pots are found filled with wine (6.26.1–2). The people of Andros, adds Pausanias, say that at their festival of Dionysos wine flows of its own accord from the temple. In a myth about the origin of a festival of Dionysos at Tyre the newly invented wine is described by the god as a 'spring' (Chapter 9). In the classical period Greek women were normally discouraged from drinking wine. But in Euripides' *Bacchae* (707; cf. 142) Dionysos creates from the earth a spring of wine for his female followers ('maenads'). There are magic vines that produce mature grapes in a single day (Sophokles fragment 253), and Apulian vase-paintings depict wine flowing directly from grapes (Chapters 6 and 7).

Third, despite its communality the Anthesteria contained secret rituals, performed by a band of women, that included sacrifice, an oath, and the sexual union between Dionysos and the wife of the 'king'. These female rituals have been connected, albeit controversially, with a series of fifth-century BC Athenian vase-paintings that show women performing ritual around an image of Dionysos (e.g. Figure 3) and sometimes ladling wine from a large container into cups as an offering to the god. A fragmentary text discovered on papyrus associates the invention of wine with Dionysiac mystic initiation (*TrGF* II 646a). To the performance of secret Dionysiac ritual at the heart of a communal festival, and to the use of wine in mystery-cult, we will return in Chapter 5.

Fourth, the Anthesteria was not the festival of unmitigated joy that we might expect of a wine festival. Several elements of it embody death or pollution. For instance, a myth associated with the festival was that Dionysos first revealed the vine and wine-making to an Attic peasant called Ikarios, who shared the wine with his neighbours. But on drinking the wine they thought themselves poisoned, and killed Ikarios. His daughter Erigone consequently hanged herself, and this hanging was commemorated in the swinging of Athenian girls at the Anthesteria. In the *Odyssey* we find not only the use of wine in the

Figure 3 Attic kylix painted by Makron.

Source: Berlin, Antikensammlung, Staatliche Museen zu Berlin. Reproduced by permission of bpk Berlin, photo by Ingrid Geske-Heiden.

burial of Achilles (see above, p. 16), but also – and more relevantly to the Ikarios story – instances of the power of wine to engender death (11.61) and violence (21.295–301). According to Plutarch (*Moralia* 655) the Athenians at the Anthesteria used to 'pour a libation of the wine before drinking it and pray that the use of the medicine would be harmless and safe for them'. In poetry of the sixth century BC it is said that Dionysos gave to humankind wine as a 'joy and burden' (*Shield* 400; *Catalogue of Women* fragment 239).

And so even in wine, as in other gifts of Dionysos (notably mystery-cult), there is ambivalence. One explanation given of Dionysos' cult epithet *dimorphos*, 'dual-formed', is that drunkenness can produce joy or irascibility (Diodorus 4.5.2). Drinking unmixed wine could cause madness (Herodotus 6.84). But ritual must end well, and the moderate practice of drinking wine mixed with water at the Anthesteria was – we may infer from remarks by the historians of Attica Phanodemos and Philochoros – envisaged as commemorating the introduction of the practice by Dionysos himself. Dionysos is invoked by Plato's Socrates to help his search for the good in the well-mixed life (*Philebus* 61c). Plato's discussion of the role of wine in the city is pervaded by a sense of its power for good or evil, and Dionysos is associated with the control of unruliness (*Laws* 671e1). The ambivalence of Dionysos I have already touched on in the first chapter, and to his association with death I will return in the sixth.

Initiation into the Eleusinian mysteries culminated in the revelation – to those being initiated ('initiands') – of an ear of corn, and the ceremony also celebrated Demeter's bestowal of corn on humankind. Demeter presides both over the growth of corn from the earth and over the ritual that ensures the happiness beneath the earth of those who have been initiated ('initiates'). Post-mortem happiness is embodied not only in ritual (a mere human construction) but also in *nature*, in the *re-emergence* from the earth of what sustains human life (corn) and can only be the gift of a deity. An inscription from second-century AD Egypt expresses the decision of a man not to weep for his dead daughter, given the comfort he finds in the changing seasons: Winter offers the dead girl milk, olives and the narcissus, Spring honey and the rose, and Summer the drink of Bacchos and a crown of grapes. The wine drunk in Dionysiac mystic initiation was probably represented as a gift for humankind from Dionysos. In *Bacchae* Teiresias pairs Demeter and Dionysos as 'the two first things among humans': Demeter nourishes them with dry food, Dionysos with wine (274–9). Wine does not sustain life to the extent that corn does, but it does embody – in nature and not merely in ritual – the transformation or liberation of the psyche. The wine that the god makes flow miraculously is an extreme expression of its belonging to nature: the mediation of human labour is not required. In sixth-century vase-painting this belonging of wine to nature is sometimes expressed by Dionysos drinking wine not from a cup but from an animal horn.

VEGETATION

The vine is not the only plant with which Dionysos is associated. In *Bacchae* he pulls the top of a tall fir-tree to the ground, sets Pentheus on the branches, and releases the tree so that Pentheus is left conspicuously high up on it (1064–75). The maenads then uproot the tree and tear Pentheus apart. Five centuries later Pausanias reports that two images of Dionysos at Corinth were made from this very tree: the Delphic oracle had ordered the Corinthians to find the tree and 'worship it equally with the god' (2.2.7). At about the same time Maximus of Tyre writes that 'the peasants honour Dionysos by planting in the field an uncultivated tree-trunk, a rustic statue' (2.1). And according to Plutarch (*Moralia* 675) all Greeks sacrifice to Dionysos as tree god (*Dendrites*). He is also associated with fruit and flowers. From the classical period onwards Greek texts associate Dionysos with the personified Seasons, and in the mosaics and on the sarcophagi of late antiquity Dionysos seems to symbolise, along with the Seasons, the cycle of the rebirth of nature. Plutarch also states (*Moralia* 365) that the Greeks regard Dionysos as the master not only of wine but of every kind of 'liquid growth', and quotes the words of Pindar: 'May joyful Dionysos swell the fruit of the trees, the pure light of harvest.'

ANIMALS

Dionysos is frequently associated with domesticated animals and with wild ones (notably the leopard). The most spectacular embodiment of this association was in the great procession staged in Alexandria by Ptolemy II Philadelphus (king of Egypt 282–246 BC), in which the triumphal return of Dionysos from India included numerous exotic animals, as well as Dionysos himself reclining on a statue of an elephant directed by a satyr on its neck. The god has a unique rapport with those beasts that are uncontrollable by humans. As early as the sixth century BC his chariot is shown (in vase-painting) drawn by wild animals.

Dionysos is not only associated but often actually *identified* with animals (just as he is both associated and identified with wine). In the *Homeric Hymn to Dionysos* not only does he create a vine (and ivy), and a shaggy bear: he himself turns into a roaring lion. The chorus of *Bacchae* call on Dionysos: 'appear as a bull or a many-headed snake or a fire-blazing lion for us to see' (1017–9). To the daughters of Minyas 'he became bull and lion and leopard' (Antoninus Liberalis 10). The women of Elis, according to Plutarch (*Moralia* 299b), call on him to come as a bull (Chapter 4). In *Bacchae* Dionysos seems to Pentheus to be a bull (921–2). And in myth he is occasionally transformed into a goat.

It is not only Dionysos but also his followers who are associated and identified with animals. Maenads are sometime represented with wild animals, frequently as wearing the skins of fawns or leopards, occasionally as suckling wild animals (*Bacchae* 699–702), and occasionally as eating raw flesh (together with wearing fawnskins at *Bacchae* 137–9). Eating raw flesh, which distinguishes animals from humans, assimilated the maenads of myth to animals: a brief reference in an inscription from Miletos (276 BC) suggests that some meat may have been actually eaten raw in Dionysiac cult, albeit not necessarily with the savagery that it symbolised. Dionysos himself could be called *ōmēstes*, 'Eater of Raw Flesh'.

The male followers of Dionysos known as satyrs have some animal characteristics, notably nakedness and a horse tail. Originally, it seems, they were unconnected with Dionysos (Hesiod fragment 123), but in the sixth century BC became part of his retinue, as did the somewhat similar silens, with the result that 'satyr' and 'silen' were used interchangeably. Men or boys dress up (or rather down) as satyrs. The vase-paintings of the ship-cart containing Dionysos and satyrs playing pipes were no doubt inspired by the annual ritual enactment, at the Anthesteria, of a mythical event (the arrival of Dionysos) by men dressed as satyrs. This kind of impersonation was a precursor of drama (Chapter 7). At the Great Dionysia men dressed as satyrs to be a chorus in satyric drama. And in mystery-cult you might become a satyr, or a ram, a bull, a kid (Chapter 5).

Satyrs combine humanity, animality, and immortality. To dress up as a satyr is to acquire another identity, as an immortal creature in the presence of Dionysos, by means of collapsing all three fundamental categories of living being into one: human, animal, and deity. Moreover, the satyrs are creatures of the wild who nevertheless belong to the heart of the polis. And just as Dionysos yokes wild beasts to his chariot, and civilises the practice of wine-drinking, so in satyric drama the satyrs are frequently present at the transformation of nature into culture, at the first ever extraction of wine from grapes (Sophokles *Dionysiskos*) or of lyrical sound from a dead tortoise (Sophokles *Ichneutai*).

Finally, nature itself joins in Dionysiac cult. From a rock, struck by a maenad with her *thrysos*, a stream of water 'leaps out' (705 *ekpēdai*), like the leaping (*pēdan*) of the maenads and Dionysos in the dance. When they are possessed, maenads draw milk and honey from the rivers (Plato *Ion* 534a). And when on Mt. Kithairon they moved their *thyrsoi* and invoked their god, 'the whole mountain and the wild animals joined in the bacchanal, and nothing remained unmoved in running' (*Bacchae* 724–7). In the paean to Bakchos (another name for Dionysos) by Philodamos (inscribed at Delphi in 340–39 BC) all immortals and all mortals rejoice at the birth of Dionysos, and the earth revels and dances.

OVERVIEW

We have seen that the association of Dionysos with nature is not indiscriminate. It is not so much with the agricultural or the pastoral, with cereal crops or herds of animals, as with those elements of nature that are dangerous: wild animals, and the fruit of the vine. Wine is dangerous, but also seems to re-unite what makes humankind unique – the consciousness that accompanies the subjection of nature – with what grows out of the earth. This synthesis of culture with nature is expressed in the hybrid form of the satyr. It is also to be found – as the transformation of human identity – in the various activities of Dionysos prefigured in this chapter (in our description of the Anthesteria) and described more fully in what follows.

3

COMMUNALITY

INTRODUCTION

By communality I mean the sum of the feelings and actions of several individuals that promote and express their simultaneous belonging to the same group. Communality is greatly facilitated when people are gathered into the same place. Consumer capitalism disintegrates the emotional wholeness of communality. In our large-scale societies the intense emotion that may be generated by a gathering of people into the same place can seem strangely insignificant and powerless, for significance and power always seem to be elsewhere.

The Greek polis of the classical period was more self-contained – economically and politically – than the modern nation-state, and a large proportion of its inhabitants could be gathered into one place. And so communality might be emotionally self-contained and politically significant. The overwhelming power to inspire communality, whether in the whole polis or in a small group, was ascribed in particular to Dionysos. And because communality breaks down individual self-containment and may replace it with a sense of wholeness, Dionysos is – more than any other Greek deity – imagined as actually *present*. His presence may itself be a focus and an agent of communality. But communality is so powerful that here again, as we shall see, the Dionysiac is dangerously ambivalent.

DIONYSOS IN HOMER

There are in Homer only three brief mentions of Dionysos and a single brief narration of a myth involving him. The myth is of his persecution by the Thracian king Lykourgos (*Iliad* 6.130–40). Remarkably, and in contrast to most other myths of human resistance to Dionysos (and even to later versions of this one), the king defeats the god, who flees terrified into the sea. And then Zeus, not Dionysos, punishes Lykourgos.

It used to be thought that Dionysos was rare in Homer because a new arrival, not yet established in the Greek pantheon. This explanation then lost its attraction with the discovery of the god's name in texts from the bronze age (Chapter 2). Further, Dionysos is not just rare in Homer but (in the Lykourgos story) *weak*. The marginality of Dionysos is *ideological*. It belongs to a view of the world that, consciously or unconsciously, expresses the interests of a social group, in this case the aristocratic clan, whose ideas of heroism and glory are far removed from work on the land. All narrative involves selection, and all selection involves judgement of what is important. Homeric epic tends to exclude not only Dionysos but also (for instance) mystery-cult, agricultural work, communal festivals, and the agricultural deity Demeter. It also tends to exclude the city-state (polis). Dionysos is a god of mystery-cult, of viticulture, of the communal festival, and of the polis. Small wonder then that he is not prominent in Homer.

This is not to say that Dionysos mattered only to those who worked on the land. We have seen a rustic Dionysos bringing wine to the aristocratic wedding of Peleus and Thetis, and he was honoured in aristocratic drinking parties. But a feature of Dionysos that may not have appealed to some aristocrats was his *inclusiveness*, his association with the celebrations of a *whole* community.

DIONYSOS AND THE POLIS

In Euripides' *Bacchae* it is the polis as a whole to which Dionysos brings his cult (39–40), he will display his divinity 'to the Thebans' (48), and 'the whole land will dance' (114). According to Teiresias, 'it is from everybody that he wants to have honours in common, and to be magnified while distinguishing nobody' (209–10). 'Nobody', says Dionysos in a satyr-play by Aeschylus (*Theoroi*), 'neither young nor old is willingly absent from my choruses.'

Moving on to the fourth century BC, an oracular response insists that Dionysos be worshipped by the Athenian citizens 'all mixed up together' (Demosthenes *Meidias* 52), and Plato in discussing choruses of Dionysos refers to 'the necessity for every man and child, free and slave, female and male, and the whole polis to charm itself, the whole polis, with song . . .' (*Laws* 665). A Hellenistic epitaph from Miletos for a Dionysiac priestess refers to her going in procession 'before the whole polis'. The Greek queen of Egypt, Arsinoe, was said to have referred to the participants in a Dionysiac festival as an 'all-mixed-up mob (*pammigēs*) mob' (Athenaeus 276c).

A community, especially a polis, needs to express its unity, to make itself visible, to itself and to others. And so Dionysiac festivals were very common and remarkably persistent. For instance St. Augustine (AD 354–430) writes about the public nature of bacchic cult (in North Africa), with leading men of the city 'moving in a bacchic frenzy through the streets of the city' (*Ep.*17.4).

Indeed, the Dionysiac festival is in a sense still alive, most notably in the form of a traditional carnival that is still celebrated every February on the remote Greek island of Skyros. The whole community (and many visitors) gather in the town to see males dancing through the streets with their heads entirely covered in goatskins, wearing jangling bells, and accompanied by other males (or recently sometimes females) dressed as young women ('Korelles') or as foreigners ('Frangi'). Of course this lacks crucial elements of a Dionysiac festival (the god himself, for instance, is nowhere to be found), but it is worth noting that it is structured by the three basic combinations of opposites – man–animal, male–female, Greek–foreigner – that are fundamental also to the identities, in *Bacchae*, of Dionysos and his followers. In the ancient Athenian Anthesteria, also celebrated in February, males dressed up as animal-like satyrs, and Dionysos was escorted into the centre of the town in a cart shaped like a ship. Similarly in the Skyros festival a cart shaped like a ship moves from harbour to main square, where satirical verses on local people and issues are delivered from the ship-cart (so too at the Athenian Anthesteria participants were mocked by men on carts).

At the Anthesteria, and the rural Dionysia, even slaves participated. We are told that for the duration of the City Dionysia prisoners were released from gaol, and that at the same festival the freeing of slaves was announced in the theatre (Aeschines 3.41). Dionysos releases from imprisonment (*Bacchae* 443–7, 498, 649; Pausanias 9.16.6), and in the dreams of slaves cult for Dionysos signifies freedom (Artemidorus 2.37). Even to chained slaves he brings rest (Tibullus 1.7.41–2). Plutarch (*Moralia* 613c) and Aelius Aristides (2.331 Keil) state that he releases from everything. At Eretria (308 BC) his cult was deployed to celebrate the liberation of the city, and at Athens (294 BC) the liberator Demetrius Poliorkētēs was associated with Dionysos. The association of the Italian agricultural god Liber with freedom (*liber* means 'free') favoured his identification with Dionysos, an identification that must have contributed to the popularity of this Graeco-Roman deity throughout the Roman empire. Augustine (*City of God* 6.9) reports the view that Liber gets his name from liberating (relieving) males from semen in sexual intercourse.

Another aspect of this power of Dionysos to bring people together is the promotion of *peace*. He 'loves Peace who gives wealth' (*Bacchae* 419–20). As early as about 600 BC a sanctuary of Zeus, Hera, and Dionysos was – it seems – common to the rival cities of Lesbos (Akaios fragment 129). And as late as the first century AD Diodorus maintains that Dionysos 'in general resolved conflicts between peoples and cities, and created concord and much peace in place of civil conflicts and wars' (3.64.7).

The association of Dionysos with freedom and communality derives, in part, from his association with wine. He liberates psychologically through wine (*Bacchae* 279–83, Plutarch *Moralia* 68d, 716b), and wine tends to dissolve barriers between people. Sparta in the classical period may have been an exception. In Plato's *Laws* (637b) the Spartan Megillus declares that there are no drinking parties in Sparta, and that any Spartiate would punish any public drunkenness that he came across: a Dionysiac festival, he adds, would not be the excuse that it is at Athens, or at the Spartan colony Taras (in southern Italy) where he had seen the entire polis drunk at a festival of Dionysos. Collective drunkenness at the Anthesteria is implied also by Aristophanes (*Acharnians* 1000–2, *Frogs* 217–9).

But the Athenian Anthesteria also included, along with this Dionysiac communality, *the enactment of its opposite*, namely the isolation of the individual that is implicit in two myths associated with the festival. Because the polluted Orestes had once participated in the drinking, then and thereafter each participant drank his equal draught separately and in silence (Euripides *Iphigeneia in Tauris* 947–60). And when Ikarios distributed wine (newly given by Dionysos) among his neighbours, they thought that they had been poisoned and killed him. The consequent suicide of his daughter Erigone was commemorated at the Anthesteria.

THE RETURN OF HEPHAISTOS

The most poignant expression of the power of Dionysos and his wine to create social integration is the myth of the Return of Hephaistos. The craftsman god Hephaistos was hurled out of Olympos by his mother Hera for his deformity, and took revenge by sending her a throne with invisible fetters by which she was held fast. Only Hephaistos could release her, but he refused to return. But Dionysos made him drunk, set him on a mule, and brought him back to Olympos. In one version a precondition for Hephaistos' return is his marriage with Aphrodite. In another Dionysos is rewarded by being made one of the Olympian gods. In the aristocratic ideology embodied in Homeric epic, just as the marginality of Dionysos and of Demeter reflects the inferior status of agriculture, so the inferior status of Hephaistos reflects the inferior status of craftsmanship. But craftsmen are necessary, and so their political exclusion threatens the community.

The jovial return of Hephaistos is a frequent theme of Attic vase-painting. It is in fact the *only* identifiable myth depicted in Attic black-figure (i.e. early) vase-painting in which Dionysos plays a central role. On the 'François Vase' Kleitias depicted not only the rustic Dionysos at the wedding of Peleus and Thetis (Chapter 2) but also the return of Hephaistos, in a little procession that consists of ithyphallic satyrs, nymphs, and Hephaistos on an ithyphallic mule, and is led by Dionysos towards the Olympian deities. One of the satyrs carries a full wineskin on his back and another plays pipes. This seems to embody the power of Dionysos and his wine to integrate into a single group (on Olympos) vital but potentially marginalised or centrifugal people such as rustics and craftsmen: social integration is expressed in the (ritual) processional integration of space.

Such integration cannot be achieved by Ares (i.e. violence), who in a written version of the myth fails to force Hephaistos back, and in Kleitias' picture sits dejected while Athena gestures towards him with one hand and to the successful procession with the other. Perhaps she means to contrast them, thereby expressing the civic values with which she is often associated.

Kleitias' depiction was – it has recently been argued (Hedreen in *Journal of Hellenic Studies* 2004) – influenced by the visually impressive Dionysiac processions that were often characterised by obscenity as well as sometimes envisaged as escorting Dionysos into the community after initial rejection: for instance it was said that the Athenians' initial rejection of the original arrival of Dionysos Eleuthereus caused them a disease of the male genitals, of which they could be cured only by honouring the god, and so at the festival of Dionysos Eleuthereus, the 'City Dionysia', phalluses were carried in the great procession. Both Hephaistos and Dionysos return in a phallic procession after being rejected.

The rejection may express – among other things – hostility to a marginal group. However, the arrival of an outsider may, because he belongs to no faction and provides a focus for everybody, unite a divided community – whether the arrival is of an alien legislator or the epiphany of a god (Chapter 4) or the triumph of a man. At Patrai a communal festival of Dionysos *Aisymnetes* (a title implying impartial power over all) was founded on his arrival as an 'alien' (*xenikos*) deity (Pausanias 7.19–21). In the early sixth century BC Solon, appointed by the Athenians to resolve impartially the discord between rich and poor, was said to have called in an outsider, Epimenides, to purify the city. Kleitias' painting dates from a time not long after Solon introduced measures that included the return of impoverished exiles and citizenship for immigrant craftsmen (such as vase-painters). In

Solon's poetry Athena both protects Athens against the destruction threatened by internal conflict (1.3–4) and is associated with craftsmanship along with Hephaistos (13.49–50).

The story of Hephaistos' return was told, probably slightly earlier, by the lyric poet Alkaios of Lesbos. Another myth in which Dionysos appears in the sixth century BC, the Gigantomachy (gods fighting the giants), again shows him as integrated into the (*military*) company of deities, in their successful struggle to create the current order of the universe (confirmed also by the union of Peleus with Thetis, for a son of *Zeus* by Thetis would have overthrown his father). And Dionysos is also depicted being conducted (like Herakles) to Olympos. In Homer, by contrast, Dionysos had been weak and marginal, with no presence on Olympos.

THE THIASOS

We have seen that Dionysos may require worship from the whole, undivided community. Moreover, he is unique among the gods in the extent to which he is accompanied by a cortege, his thiasos. The chorus of *Bacchae* consist of a thiasos of his female adherents known as *mainades* ('frenzied women') or *bakchai*. They are from Lydia, but the Theban women worshipping Dionysos on the mountainside are also described as forming three thiasoi (680). Among the first words uttered by the chorus-thiasos are

> Blessed is the one who, truly happy,
> knowing the initiations of the gods,
> is pure in life and
> joins his soul to the thiasos (*thiaseuetai psūchān*) (72–6).

Mystic initiation merges the individual soul into the group. Dionysiac frenzy is 'shared' (Plato *Symposium* 218b). The objective aspect of this subjective solidarity is manifest in the descriptions, later in the play, of the maenads on the mountainside. Springing all to their feet out of sleep, they are 'a marvel of good order' (692–4). When they call with one voice on their god, the whole mountain and the animals and everything else join in their movement (725–7). Many are the museums that contain vase-paintings of maenads (sometimes with their mythical male counterparts the satyrs) moving with the para-doxical cohesion of an ecstatic group. What is remarkable about the maenads in *Bacchae* is the cohesion of the group both with nature (Chapter 2) and with itself. They run 'raised like birds' (748), i.e. with the miraculous cohesion of a flock of birds leaving the ground. Although the vine embodies the mysterious power of nature to dissolve boundaries, it is made clear in *Bacchae* (686) that these maenads are *not* drunk. Although wine is his gift to humankind, Dionysos can, even without it, dissolve the boundaries of the soul.

This psychic cohesion, or group consciousness, of the maenads in *Bacchae* is all the more striking for its contrast with the obstinate rejection of the Dionysiac by the 'tyrant' Pentheus. For much of the drama the individualism of Pentheus is absolute, the boundaries of his psyche are impermeable, and so he remains oddly unaware of the miraculous power of Dionysos that is obvious to everybody else. Rejecting Dionysos, he remains isolated, just as it is only when separated from Dionysos that the thiasos of Lydian maenads falls to the ground and disintegrates, each member into 'isolated desolation' (609). The unity of the thiasos seems to require a sense of the presence of the deity, perhaps even of the deity *possessing* the souls of the group (Chapter 8).

Bacchae ended with Dionysos introducing his cult to Thebes, and much of what takes place in the drama is a projection of this cult back into the mythical past. *Bacchae* dramatises the 'aetiological myth' of the cult, the myth that explains the foundation and the practises of the cult. Dionysos wants everybody to participate (208); eventually 'the whole polis was made bacchic' (1295), and this prefigures the Dionysiac festival as it will be practised. Another actual practice pre-figured by *Bacchae* is 'maenadism', the gathering together of women for the kind of frenzied dance, sometimes in the presence of Dionysos, that we see frequently depicted in Athenian vase-painting of the fifth century BC, when Athenian women would gladly gather at a place of Bacchic revelry (Aristophanes *Lysistrata* 1–3).

Hardly anything is known of this practice at Thebes. But in various other Greek city-states it even took the form, as in *Bacchae*, of maenads leaving the city for the mountainside. An inscription records the bringing of three maenads from Thebes to Magnesia in Ionia in the second quarter of the third century BC. From Hellenistic Miletos one inscription commemorates a woman who led a group of *bakchai* (maenads) 'to the mountain', and another (of 276 BC) specifies the privileges of the 'public' (*dēmosios*) thiasos and the public priestess of Dionysos as well as referring to the formation of other (presumably private) thiasoi. In the first century BC Diodorus (4.3) reports that it was in his time a general practice for bands of women to gather together to sacrifice and to hymn the presence of Dionysos in imitation of his ancient companions the maenads.

Why should women gather together on the mountainside? The polis is composed of separate households, a structure that is most conspicuously embodied in the tendency for each woman to be confined to the domestic sphere. And so for her to leave her separate household (in some versions, as in *Bacchae*, specifically her *loom*) so as to transcend the boundaries, both physical and psychic, between herself and other women and between herself and nature – this is a symbolic reversal of the civilised structure of the polis.

But this reversal of the structure of the polis is also the most conspicuous possible expression of its communality. The polis contains a tension between adherence to the polis and adherence to the household. In the symbolic expression of this tension in myth and ritual, adherence to the household is best symbolised by those who in reality adhere almost exclusively to it, the women. Hence the mythical *resistance* of the women to Dionysos, their unwillingness to leave the parental or marital household for his collective cult. Dionysos overcomes the resistance (in the daughters of Minyas, the daughters of Proitos, the women of Thebes) by inspiring frenzy in them. Hence also the ruthlessness with which Dionysos imposes frenzied self-destruction (kin-killing) on the ruling family that vainly resists his communal cult, a theme which in the communal Dionysiac genre of tragedy extends to myths that do not contain Dionysos (Chapter 7).

THE TENSION BETWEEN COMMUNALITIES

The symbolic importance of women in Dionysiac festivals does not mean that they excluded males. In *Bacchae*, and elsewhere, the entire polis must participate. This implies a contradiction. In *Bacchae*, which dramatises an aetiological myth of Dionysiac cult, on the one hand the whole polis participates, but on the other hand the celebrations of the maenads on the mountainside are secret (1109). The apparent contradiction corresponds in fact to a feature of Dionysiac festivals, some of which contain the participation of the whole polis but also, at the heart of the celebrations, a secret ritual performed by a group of women (Chapter 5). I will be arguing that a development of this phenomenon, the *opening up* of the mystic ritual to the whole polis at the City Dionysia, was a factor in the genesis of tragedy (Chapter 7).

But the contradiction also points to a potential ambiguity in the communality inspired by Dionysos. Communal feeling in a whole community is clearly valuable as a source of strength and cohesion, but in an initiated group within that community it may have the opposite effect – by providing a focus of loyalty that conflicts, or seems to conflict, with loyalty to the wider community. And clearly the relatively disorganised communality of the Dionysiac festival is quite different from the ecstatic coherence of the Dionysiac thiasos, and both of them are quite different from the hedonistic decorum presided over by Dionysos at the respectable symposium.

In roughly the same period as *Bacchae* there is evidence for Athenian hostility to, and sometimes persecution of, certain cults that were of foreign origin or at least imagined to be in some way foreign. These cults tended to be ecstatic and initiatory, and the hostility to them seems to have been based on the same kind of moral objection – for instance to drunkenness and sexual licence – as was advanced against the new foreign ecstatic initiatory cult by Pentheus in *Bacchae*. But we may suspect that in most such cases the basic motivation is the need felt by the centre for social cohesion, for *control*.

Of these supposedly foreign cults, those of Cybele and of Sabazios were closely associated with Dionysos, and the cults of Adonis, Cybele, and Sabazios were entirely or largely confined to women. The courtesan Phryne was prosecuted for forming thiasoi of men and women and introducing a new god called *Isodaitēs*, a name which means something like 'Equal divider in the feast' and reappears much later as a title of Dionysos (Plutarch *Moralia* 389a5; compare *Bacchae* 421–3). The appeal of foreign spirits to marginal groups, and especially to women, has been anthropologically documented. But that Dionysos appealed to women because of his imagined Asian provenance was less likely than the reverse. The imagined foreign provenance of Dionysos and of his cult, as expressed notably in *Bacchae*, may derive from the alienation of women from the deities of the male-dominated polis, as well as from the consequent male hostility to the cult, from the adoption of foreign elements such as Phrygian music, and from the aetiological myth of the annual *entry* of Dionysos into the city (Chapter 4).

There is a significant difference between on the one hand unregulated and disreputable cults such as those of Sabazios and *Isodaitēs* and on the other those that, whatever their aetiological myth or early history, in the historical period were official cults of the polis. In unregulated cult a male priest may be imagined (e.g. by Pentheus) to seduce and corrupt women, but Dionysos is an Olympian and a central god of the polis. The centrifugal tendency of maenadism is incorporated into the polis and, by becoming a temporary and merely symbolic reversal of the structure of the polis, may even reinforce its coherence. *Bacchae* dramatises this incorporation, and prefigures the enactment of secret female ritual in a polis festival of both genders (Chapter 5).

Another kind of public control is illustrated by the Milesian inscribed law of 276 BC, which requires anybody founding a thiasos to pay a fee to the public priestess. But the best extant example of contradiction between state and secret Dionysiac cult is the suppression in Italy in 186 BC of Dionysiac-initiated groups that seemed to be a conspiracy threatening the Roman state (see Chapter 5).

COMMUNALITY AND THE AUTOCRAT

We will in Chapter 5 also describe an example of state control of private thiasoi from third-century BC Egypt, where the state was a *monarchy*.

In *Bacchae* the opponent of the Dionysiac thiasos is an autocrat. Teiresias tries to persuade Pentheus to accept the new god by saying 'you rejoice when a throng stands at the gates, and the polis magnifies the name of Pentheus; he too (i.e. Dionysos), I think, takes pleasure in being honoured' (319–21). The 'tyrant' Pentheus has been treated like a god, processionally escorted – like Dionysos – into the city. But now it seems inevitable that Dionysos will usurp Pentheus' central position in the festival. An egalitarian function of the gods in Athenian democracy, and especially of Dionysos, was, by providing a focus for communal devotion, to deny it to any human individual.

However, Athenian democracy, having emerged from tyranny at the end of the sixth century BC, was by the time of *Bacchae* again fearful of a tyrannical coup, and was eventually conquered by the Macedonian monarchy. And a generation after this conquest the Athenians greeted the powerful Macedonian Demetrius Poliorkētēs as if he were a god (Chapter 4). As a focus for communal celebration, Dionysos is in the Athenian democracy imagined as subversive of autocracy, but for this very reason may in an actual autocracy be appropriated by the autocrat.

In the prologue of *Bacchae* Dionysos claims to have introduced his cult – and set people dancing – throughout Asia as far as Bactria, and threatens Pentheus with military action (21, 52). He was in fact not without military experience, having fought with the gods against the giants. Subsequently, not long after the conquest of India by Alexander the Great, Dionysos too was said (by the influential historian Cleitarchus) to have conquered India, with the result that Alexander could be imagined as having imitated Dionysos. In the great procession of king Ptolemy II Philadelphus in Alexandria, the triumphal return of Dionysos from India was enacted in such a way as to suggest not only his association with Alexander's conquests but also the association of both the divine and the human conqueror with the Ptolemies. Dionysos' triumph became a popular theme of literature and visual art, and as a symbol of universal joy persisted into nineteenth-century Germany (Chapter 10).

Although there is no good evidence that Alexander himself was during his lifetime identified with Dionysos, many of the successors to his empire – the monarchs of Egypt (the Ptolemies), Syria (the

Seleukids) and Pergamon (the Attalids) – were interested in promoting, controlling, and associating themselves with Dionysiac cult. The monarch might be assimilated to – or even identified with – the god. The attraction of Dionysos to these monarchs consisted not just in the revelry (or even the eternal happiness) associated with the god, but primarily in the idea of Dionysos as the victor (Chapter 4) who unites the whole community – under the rule of the monarch. Even the all-conquering Roman Mark Antony entering a city was welcomed as 'Dionysos' by the whole community (Chapter 4). The Roman emperors too – as successors of the Hellenistic monarchs – could be identified with Dionysos. Caligula, for instance, was said to have been named 'new Dionysos' and to have dressed as the god (Athenaeus 148d), and in an inscription from Ancyra (Chapter 7) Hadrian is acclaimed as 'New Dionysos'.

OVERVIEW

We have described the communality inspired by Dionysos in polis and thiasos. Given the interest that Greek myth, and even ritual, shows in negotiating contradiction, Dionysiac communality is some-times shown in contradiction, with individual isolation or with the communality of another group. And it is a paradox that Dionysiac communality seems to derive from the power of an individual, Dionysos, who may – from the early Hellenistic period – be replaced by a human autocrat.

4

EPIPHANY

INTRODUCTION

An inscription of the third century AD refers to 'the most *epiphanēs* god Dionysos Euboulēs', i.e. most manifest, or most given to epiphany. Epiphany occurs when deity (or its manifestations) is perceived by one or more of the senses. It will include for instance even the arrival of a statue of a deity in a procession, in so far as the onlookers imagine themselves to be seeing the deity.

Of all Greek deities it is Dionysos who most tends to manifest himself among humankind, and to do so in various forms (Chapter 2). Plato calls him (along with the Muses and Apollo) a *suneortastās*, 'companion of the festival' (*Laws* 653d). To his kidnappers in the *Homeric Hymn to Dionysos* he appears as a lion. The miraculous appearance of ivy or vine, or of wine, may seem to indicate his *presence*, or even his embodiment in what appears. He may be thought to be present within his worshippers (Chapter 8). Although there is 'no god more present (*praesentior*)' than Dionysos (Ovid *Metamorphoses* 3.658–9), he may be invisible to those who do not accept him (Euripides *Bacchae* 500–2). Our task is to decide what the various forms of Dionysos' presence mean, and how they relate to each other.

RITUAL AND CRISIS

Epiphanies tend to occur in certain contexts. Two such contexts are ritual and crisis. An example of a *ritual* epiphany is the advent of Dionysos (impersonated, or as his statue) in a procession at an annual festival, for instance at the Anthesteria (Chapter 2). The *crisis* may occur in myth (e.g. the capture of Dionysos by pirates) or in the present (e.g. Theseus helping Athens in the battle of Marathon). These may seem to be opposites, in that ritual epiphanies generally belong to an ordered timetable, whereas the crisis and its epiphany are essentially unpredictable. However, the two contexts are both occasions for the enactment of human control over disorder. Ritual may in fact be performed in a crisis, or contain its own crisis.

Ritual is the manifestation of traditional stereotypical action in the face of potential disorder or of (as in a crisis) actual disorder. The absorbing manifestation (dramatisation) of order in ritual may, even if only symbolic, be a model and a focus for reversing the debilitating disintegration of the group or indeed of the individual. This mysterious saving power of ritual to create coherence, to inspire the centre against disintegration, is easily imagined as issuing from the central presence (epiphany) of a single all-powerful individual, a deity bringing salvation. In some crises ritual is used to create a saving epiphany, and in some crises the danger (or human power-lessness) is such that an epiphany occurs without the performance of ritual.

In other words the two main contexts of epiphany – ritual and crisis – interpenetrate. In both of them epiphany may occur in response to invocation. Even the annual processional epiphany may evoke crisis: for example, the advent of Dionysos in a ship-cart at the Anthesteria seems to have evoked the epiphany of Dionysos when he was captured by pirates (Chapter 2). The processional epiphany may also be deployed and adapted to resolve an unpredictable situation of crisis: the first known instance of this is the escort of Peisistratus into Athens by a tall young woman dressed as Athena (Herodotus 1.60). Much later, the people of Ephesos called Mark Antony 'Dionysos' as they escorted him into their city (Plutarch, *Life of Antony* 24). In these last two instances a processional epiphany is deployed to establish or accommodate the (dangerous) power of a mortal – an issue to which I will shortly return.

THE EPIPHANIES IN EURIPIDES' *BACCHAE*

In *Bacchae* the chorus' reference to themselves as conducting (85 *katagousai*) Dionysos from the Phrygian mountains into the streets of Greece evokes the *Katagōgia*, the processional entry of Dionysos into a city. Dionysos has already, in the prologue, emphasised his intention to manifest himself as a god to all the Thebans (47–8), and in the course of the drama makes further epiphanies. *Bacchae* gives us unique access to various kinds of Dionysiac epiphany (as it does to other aspects of Dionysiac cult).

A ritual that may, despite its assured happy ending, create a (temporary) crisis, is mystic initiation (Chapter 5), in which a crisis of anxiety and despondency among the initiands may be reversed by the epiphany of deity bringing salvation. Some such sequence seems to have occurred in the mystery-cult at Eleusis. In *Bacchae* Dionysos is said to transmit his *orgia* (mystic ritual or mystic objects) to his priest 'face to face' (470). When he is imprisoned by king Pentheus, and his despairing followers (the chorus of maenads) invoke his presence (566, 583), he suddenly makes his appearance, accompanied by thunder and an earthquake that destroys Pentheus' house, and transforms the fear of the chorus into joy. Numerous details of this episode correspond closely to the ritual of mystic initiation (Chapter 5), including his epiphany, in which he appears as a 'light' that is welcomed by the chorus (608) but – horrifically – attacked by Pentheus (630–1). Here a ritual epiphany is projected in myth as occurring in the context of a crisis: the vulnerability of the chorus caused by the imprisonment of Dionysos.

His appearance to Pentheus takes place in the enclosed space of the royal house. Dionysos excels at epiphanies within enclosed space. We have seen an example from Elis (Chapter 2). And when the daughters of Minyas refuse to leave their house to join his cult, ivy and grape-vines appear on their looms, snakes in the baskets of wool, and milk and wine from the ceiling. This event was associated with the origin of a ritual at a festival called Agrionia at Orchomenos in Boeotia.

Although Dionysos is present, Pentheus – being impious – cannot see him (500–2). But after Pentheus is put 'out of his mind' in a 'light frenzy' (850–1), he dresses as a maenad, mysteriously changes his attitude to the new cult from aggression to fascinated docility, and sees Dionysos as a bull, whereupon Dionysos tells him that 'now you see what you ought to see' (924). Agaue becomes 'possessed' by Dionysos (1124). Maenads are *entheoi* ('having god in them': Sophokles *Antigone* 964). Plato notes that maenads 'when possessed draw honey and milk from the rivers, but not when they are in their senses' (*Ion* 534a): he compares this with poetic inspiration, for which in fact Dionysos himself is a source, as when he makes an epiphany to the Roman poet Horace (*Odes* 2.19). Philo (first century AD) writes that Bacchic worshippers get excited until they see what they long for (*On the Contemplative Life* 12).

The epiphany of a deity may emerge entirely from the framed expectant enthusiasm of ritual. In Greek vase-painting of the classical period Dionysos frequently appears in the company of frenzied women (maenads). And in the first century BC Diodorus (4.3.3) records the practice, 'in many Greek cities', of cult for Dionysos that includes married women in groups 'generally hymning the presence (*parousia*) of Dionysos, imitating the maenads who were the companions of the god'. The thiasos is a band of mortals, but also the immortal company of the god.

Pentheus is in the next scene escorted to Mt. Kithairon to spy on the maenads. The chorus sing an aggressive song that culminates in an appeal to Dionysos to come as bull or many-headed snake or fire-blazing lion, and with laughing face to throw a deadly noose around Pentheus. This reminds us of Dionysos' earlier appearance as a bull to Pentheus, and resembles invocations that we know from other texts. The women of Elis sing 'come, hero Dionysos, to the Elean pure temple, with the Graces, to the temple, rushing with your bull's foot', and then twice sing 'worthy bull, worthy bull' (Plutarch *Moralia* 299b). And from Dura Europos, a garrison town on the Euphrates, a third-century AD graffito invokes Dionysos to 'come laughing', and also seems to refer to Dionysos as *Einosis*, i.e. 'Earthquake' – the same name that Dionysos earlier in *Bacchae* invoked to shake Pentheus' house. It seems that at Dura Europos the epiphany of Dionysos was invoked as an earthquake. There were various ways and various formulae with which the thiasos, or the whole polis, might invoke or welcome the longed-for presence of Dionysos: for instance the traditional cries *Iakche* and *Dithyrambe*, or at the Athenian Lenaia festival the ritual formula 'Call the god' with the response 'Semelean Iakche giver of wealth'. Dionysos descended to the underworld through the Alkyonian lake at Lerna, and is ritually summoned up out of the water by the sound of trumpets (Chapter 6).

The ease with which Dionysos makes epiphanies goes with his constant and ubiquitous *mobility*. He does accordingly have relatively few elaborate temples. He seems more inclined to destroy buildings than to construct them. He does not, as Demeter does in the *Homeric Hymn to Demeter*, give instructions for the building of a temple. At the City Dionysia his image was brought to the (open air) *theatre*. In *Bacchae* the Theban maenads are driven from their homes to sit on 'roofless' rocks (38). An inscription from Thasos (1st century AD) dedicates to Dionysos a 'temple under the open sky . . . an evergreen cave' (31 Jaccottet).

To return to *Bacchae*. Dionysos sets Pentheus on the top of a tree and disappears. His voice is heard urging the maenads to kill Pentheus, a light of holy fire appears between heaven and earth, and there is an all-pervasive silence. After the death of Pentheus, the final epiphany takes the form of the so-called *deus ex machina*, the theatrical convention of a deity appearing at the end of a tragedy in order to bring the disordered action to an ordered conclusion by giving instructions for the future. Given the genesis of tragedy in Dionysiac cult, and the Dionysiac nature of many of its earliest themes (Chapter 7), the appearance of Dionysos here to establish his cult in Thebes and to order the exile of the surviving members of the ruling family can be seen as a (late fifth-century) instance of what had been the Dionysiac prototype of the epiphany scenes that conclude several tragedies.

EPIPHANY AND SOCIETY

The processional epiphany of Dionysos tended to celebrate the mythical first arrival of the god, and these myths often contain an episode of resistance to his arrival, as for example did the Theban myth dramatised in *Bacchae*. We have already seen (in Chapter 3) an example in the aetiological myth of the theatrical festival of Dionysos Eleuthereus (the 'City Dionysia'). Another instance is the epiphany of Dionysos in response to the resistance of the daughters of Minyas, a myth associated with ritual at Orchomenos. These myths of the dire consequences of resistance or neglect have the function of ensuring the perpetuation of the cult.

The social disintegration that results from the neglect of communal cult is often expressed in myth as *disease*. And Dionysos is often envisaged as purifier or healer, as in the passage of Sophokles quoted in the final sentence of this book. His healing power consists in the social unity achieved by communal ritual and by his status as an outsider. As we saw of Dionysos *Aisymnetes* at Patrai (Chapter 3), the alien quality of a deity who arrives from elsewhere may serve to fascinate and unite the community. A wooden mask, found in the sea off Lesbos, had something divine about it but also an alien (*xenos*) quality, and was worshipped by the local people as Dionysos (Pausanias 10.19.3).

Bacchae also gives us a sense of Dionysos as a deity who is, as we noted earlier, somehow closer to humanity than any other deity. His mother was a mere mortal, the daughter of Kadmos. Throughout most of the drama he has the form of a human being, interacting with other human beings but detectable as a god only by his devotees. In the earliest surviving narrative about him, and the only one in Homer, Dionysos flees in fear from king Lykourgos into the lap of Thetis in the sea (*Iliad* 6.136–7): unlike Aphrodite wounded in the battle before Troy, Dionysos does not escape to Olympos, but rather his flight from a mortal belongs entirely to this world.

Later, however, his apparently powerless submission (in the *Homeric Hymn* to the pirates, in *Bacchae* to king Pentheus) is transformed into its opposite by epiphany, an emotive transformation that is in some respects comparable to the release of Paul and Silas from prison in the *Acts of the Apostles* (Chapter 9). The alienated powerlessness of human beings consists both in being subjected to other human beings and in the unknowable remoteness of the power of deity. To be released from a crisis of subjection to other humans by the sudden intimate presence of Dionysos reverses simultaneously both forms of powerlessness, and so is appropriately imagined as the supreme happiness suddenly conferred by mystic ritual, especially as it occurs through a similar reversal within the figure of Dionysos himself – from powerless human prisoner to all-powerful god.

Dionysos is chased away or imprisoned by mere mortals, or just disappears (e.g. Plutarch *Moralia* 717a), but returns in triumph: he is often associated with *victory* (e.g. *kallinīkos* at *Bacchae* 1147, 1161). Indeed, the Greek word for triumph, *thriambos*, first occurs in an invocation of Dionysos (Pratinas 708 *PMG*), and is also a title of Dionysos (as well as a song). In later texts the practice of the triumphal procession is said to have originated with Dionysos (Diodorus 3.65.8; Arrian *Anabasis* 6.28.2; etc.). His entry into the community is not just an arrival. It is associated with his victory over disappearance or rejection or capture, with the unity of the community (envisaged as its 'purification' from disease), and/or with the arrival of spring, as in the following anonymous song:

> We will sing Dionysos,
> in the sacred days,
> who has been absent for twelve months.
> Present is the season (or 'his gifts'), and all the flowers (929b *PMG*).

We have seen (in Chapter 3) that it was the dissolution of democracy that allowed the epiphanic accolade to be given to *human* victors, such as the processional entry into Athens of the powerful military leader Demetrius Poliorkētēs, as a god (sang the Athenians), not made of stone or wood but real, present, and visible, unlike the other gods. They were even said to have renamed the Dionysia festival 'Demetria' in his honour (294 BC). The universal ritual welcome for the divine outsider whose epiphany brings well-being to the polis is adapted to the new political circumstances. It is because he is of all deities the most present and visible, particularly in his processional epiphany, that Dionysos may be embodied by a mere mortal.

Even the god's most famous (Indian) triumphal procession was inspired by the conquest of India by a human being, Alexander the Great. Mark Antony, entering Ephesos in 41 BC while in control of the eastern Mediterranean (41 BC), was celebrated as Dionysos at Ephesos by the 'full city' (Plutarch *Antony* 24) and at Athens by 'the Athenians and their wives and children' (Seneca *Suasoriae* 1.6). Later, when Mark Antony was in Alexandria and doomed to succumb to the advancing forces of Octavian, there were just before midnight suddenly heard music and singing and shouting and bacchic cries and the leaping of satyrs, as if a thiasos was leaving 'through the middle of the city to the gate facing the enemy'. This sign was, Plutarch adds (*Antony* 75), taken to be of Antony being abandoned by the god whom he had especially imitated and associated with. Once again, but this time to express the desperate isolation of Antony, there is evoked a celebration of the whole polis. In 'The god leaves Antony' by the Greek poet Cavafy (1863–1933) this idea is developed: the departing 'mystic thiasos' is a wonderful event that nevertheless signifies the loss of Cavafy's beloved native city of Alexandria.

PUBLIC EPIPHANY AND INTIMATE EPIPHANY

It will by now be clear that there are two kinds of Dionysiac epiphany: on the one hand the public epiphany, in which the imagined deity is the focus of the collective excitement of the whole community, and on the other the more intimate epiphany within the closed circle of the initiated thiasos. Both kinds are prefigured in the aetiological myth dramatised in *Bacchae*. And they may occur at the same festival (Chapter 5): for instance at the Anthesteria was enacted not only the public procession in which Dionysos arrived in the ship-cart but also a series of secret actions, performed by a small group of women (perhaps at the destination of the procession), in one of which the wife of the 'king' magistrate was 'given away' to Dionysos in the sacred marriage. In both these rituals, the public and the secret, the god is *present*, but we cannot say in what form – as an image or an impersonator or in some other way even more dependent on the imagination. But a famous series of Attic vase-paintings (e.g. figure 3) depicts a ritual performed by a small group of women in which the form taken by the presence of Dionysos *is* clear: it consists of a mask set on a pole or pillar that is usually clothed (this may or may not have been one of the secret female rituals performed at the Anthesteria).

What about the *male* adherents of Dionysos? At the Anthesteria the satyrs depicted playing pipes inside the ship-cart with Dionysos, who were presumably embodied by citizens, have a closer relation to the god than do the numerous other participants of the festival who dress as satyrs. In general a small group of adherents may be more intimate with the god than a whole polis. The intimacy of Dionysos with his companions, the thiasos, is a distinctive and fundamental characteristic of this god. It works at two interpenetrating levels: from the costumed human adherents of the god the imagination projects his mythical companions (satyrs, maenads or nymphs), whom the human adherents may be imagined as imitating or embodying.

At the level of myth, the earliest mention of Dionysos' companions is as his 'nurses' (intimacy indeed), who are attacked along with their god by king Lykourgos (*Iliad* 6.132–6). In *Bacchae* the thiasos of Lydian maenads is desolated by the imprisonment of their god, fearing for their own safety, and then are overcome with joy at his miraculous return. As for the mythical male thiasos (of satyrs), in the only surviving satyr-play, Euripides' *Cyclops*, the chorus of satyrs wistfully complain 'Oh dear one, dear Bacchus, where are you, off on your own, shaking your fair hair?' (73–75), and in the last line of the play they look forward, now liberated from Polyphemos, to rejoining the service of Dionysos for ever.

This intimacy between god and thiasos is visible in museums all over the world, in many of the numerous Attic vase-paintings in which Dionysos appears along with his ecstatic thiasos of maenads or satyrs (or both together). These scenes may be imagined as mythical, and yet they can hardly be *mere* fantasy. Their reflection of the level of actual human practice may even include the god himself, for ecstasy, we remember, allowed the maenads to draw milk and honey from the rivers and to see 'what they long for', and so may also, especially if combined with invocation, have allowed them – like the maenadic Pentheus 'out of his mind' and in a 'light frenzy' – to experience the epiphany of the god.

OVERVIEW

Dionysos is especially given to epiphanies. The key document for understanding them is Euripides' *Bacchae*, which dramatises an aetiological myth of his cult. The drama consists of an epiphany of the god, or rather of a series of epiphanies, both public (to the whole polis) and private (to his thiasos, or as in mystic ritual). The myth is about crises produced by resistance to the god. But these crises lead to the establishment of the cult, in which the epiphanies, which serve to unite the group (polis or thiasos), are invoked and controlled by ritual.

5

MYSTERY-CULT

INTRODUCTION: WHAT IS MYSTERY-CULT?

Mystery-cult was an important ritual for the ancient Greeks, and something like it occurs in numerous pre-modern cultures. But two factors in particular reduce its accessibility for us. It was in antiquity veiled by secrecy, and having disappeared from Europe with the triumph of Christianity it seems to have no place (or at most a very marginal place) in modern industrial society.

Mystic initiation is a rite of passage. That is to say, it is a ritual that changes fundamentally the state or status of one or more people. A rite of passage with which we are familiar is the wedding, which achieves the transition to the married state. Mystery-cult involves the incorporation (or 'initiation') of an individual into a real or imagined group which belongs at least in part to the next world. The initiand chooses to undergo a secret and frightening ritual that consists of a transition from the anxious ignorance of the outsider, through an experience that might be like death and that involves revelation (sometimes of sacred objects), into a new blissful state as an insider (initiate). As a pre-enactment of death, it might remove (as do modern near-death experiences) the fear of death.

This is inevitably a crude definition, which will not fit every instance of a kind of cult that was enacted in various places, over many centuries, and in honour of many different deities (notably Dionysos, Demeter, Isis, and Attis). However, these various mystery-cults do seem to have had a similar structure. In particular, Dionysiac mystery-cult does seem similar in certain respects to the rather better known mystery-cult of Demeter and her daughter Korē at Eleusis. But in contrast to the Eleusinian cult, which though influential belonged to a specific place, the mystery-cult of Dionysos had no single head-quarters or controlling organisation, and so in the various places and the many centuries of its performance it exhibited greater variety (and overlap with other mystery-cults) than the Eleusinian.

Given these difficulties, it is impossible to write a simple account of what happened in Dionysiac mystery-cult. What we can do is to consider the most important fragments of information, from various places and times, and emphasise certain basic and recurrent features.

To what extent did Dionysiac mystery-cult remain the same throughout the many centuries in which we have evidence for its existence? On the one hand there seem to have been significant changes in the ritual: for instance, the frequent use of the *liknon* (see below, p. 61) seems to date from the first century BC. And it seems likely that significant changes in social and political context, for instance the creation of the Greek monarchies of the Hellenistic period, would produce important changes in mystery-cult, or at least in its social significance. Dionysiac mystery-cult could be presented as a threat to the political order (*Bacchae*, Livy 39), or – perhaps in part because of its potential subversiveness – integrated into the political order (as seems implicit in several inscriptions).

On the other hand the basic identity of Dionysiac mystery-cult, as described in our first paragraph, seems to have persisted throughout most of Graeco-Roman antiquity. We will in what follows twice see Dionysiac mystery-cult described as 'ancient'. To be sure, our picture of the ritual differs in different periods. But this may be in part because in each period a different kind of evidence – whether inscriptional, dramatic, literary, philosophical, Christian, or in vase-paintings, papyri, wall-paintings, sculptural reliefs, or mosaics – tends to predominate. Despite this, continuity can even be traced in some details of the cult. An example is provided by the significance of the *belt*: in the fifth century BC attention is given to it on the initiand Pentheus (*Bacchae*), and a thousand years later it is used in mystic initiation (Proclus) and in the divinisation of a statue of Dionysos (an Orphic poem preserved by Macrobius). In between it makes numerous appearances, including visual representations of Dionysiac costume, and to designate different grades of initiates in an inscription of the second century AD (from Torre Nova).

THE FIRST FOUR CENTURIES

In our earliest surviving Greek literature, the epics of Homer, no mystery-cult of any kind is mentioned. From this it has been inferred that such cult did not exist at the time of the composition of the epics. But this is a false inference. Mystery-cult could easily have been *ignored* by Homeric epic. We have seen that Homeric heroic ideology tends to exclude and denigrate Dionysos (Chapter 3). Moreover it is part of this ideology that in the next world the hero is a gloomy and insubstantial residue of his living self – quite unlike the happiness in the next world obtained by mystic initiation. Our earliest detailed evidence for mystery-cult is the *Homeric Hymn to Demeter*, which was composed at some time between 650 and 550 BC – not (despite its name) by Homer. It narrates in detail the mythical founding of the mystery-cult at Eleusis, including Demeter's statement of its effect as ensuring its initiates a portion of good things in the next world. Some details of the narrative, such as the drinking of the special drink called *kykeōn*, clearly correspond to actions performed in the ritual of initiation at Eleusis. Ritual is projected into mythical narrative.

As for the mystery-cult of Dionysos, it has been argued (by Isler-Kerényi) that there are evocations of it in Attic vase-painting of the sixth century BC. The writings ascribed by late authors (notably Pausanias 8.37.5) to the shadowy figure of Onomacritus, who we know to have been active in Athens in the late sixth century BC, suggest the possibility – but no more than a possibility – that he may have had a hand in organising Dionysiac mystery-cult there.

For our next evidence we move to the two opposite ends of the Greek world. An inscription from Cumae in southern Italy, generally dated to the first half of the fifth century BC, forbids burial 'in this' (i.e. presumably plot of land) to any one who is not *bebakcheumenos* ('made bacchic' in some sense), i.e. probably initiated into a Dionysiac group. At the other end of the Greek world, just north of the Black Sea, the city of Olbia has yielded numerous small bone plates that seem to be tokens of having been initiated into mystery-cult. Three of them, dated to the fifth century BC, contain various inscriptions including the name of Dionysos, and the words 'life death life', 'peace war', and 'truth falsehood'. It was in Olbia that occurred, according to Herodotus (4.79), the Dionysiac initiation of the philhellene Scythian king Skyles, whose large and luxurious house was, just before his initiation, burnt to the ground by a thunderbolt sent by the god. This reminds us of the destruction of the house of Pentheus, the tyrant who rejects the establishment of Dionysiac cult in Thebes in Euripides' *Bacchae*. In both cases it seems that an imagined element of the ritual (a thunderbolt) has found its way into the narrative. *Bacchae* undoubtedly refers to mystery-cult (e.g. 72–3, 465–74). And in fact, just as the *Homeric Hymn to Demeter* is a narrative that corresponds in detail with Eleusinian initiation, so *Bacchae* dramatises a myth corresponding to Dionysiac initiation, in which the strange behaviour and experiences of Pentheus belong to a narrative projection of the anxious reluctance of the initiand. Ancient rites of passage, such as mystery-cult or the wedding, tend to allow for the expression of reluctance (by initiand or bride), so that it may eventually be overcome – in the ritual, though not necessarily in the corresponding myth. And of course the blissful conclusion of mystic ritual cannot be made public, for if it was, then the initiand would not feel the necessary terror. And so the killing of Pentheus has to be real rather than merely ritually enacted.

Bacchae is, if properly understood, invaluable evidence of the subjective experience of the Dionysiac initiand (without of course reflecting it *directly*), at least at the end of the fifth century BC. For instance, the riddling language used by Dionysos when speaking to Pentheus of mystic initiation corresponds with the riddling language used to confuse and intrigue the initiand in the initial phase of the mystic transition. Then, during his unsuccessful attempt to imprison Dionysos in the darkness of his house, Pentheus exhibits very odd behaviour, which corresponds in many details to descriptions we have of the initial anxiety of the mystic initiand. For instance, as the culmination of Pentheus' anxiety there appears a miraculous light, which he attacks with a sword, identifiying it with the god (editors, not understanding the mystic allusion, generally change the manuscript 'light' to 'apparition'). This corresponds with the mystic light (in the darkness) that brings salvation. Whereas the isolated and terrified chorus-members greet Dionysos as 'greatest light', Pentheus persists – horrifyingly – in his stubborn hostility.

Why is his persistent hostility so horrifying? Because the light appearing in the darkness transformed the ignorant suffering of the initiand into enlightened joy. And there is more to it than that. Plutarch (fragment 178) compares the experience of the soul at death to mystic initiation: he describes various agitated experiences (much like those of Pentheus) that are transformed into bliss by the appearance of a wonderful light in the darkness. This passage shows that the Greeks were aware of the similarity between mystic initiation and near-death experiences. Extensive research into near-death experiences over the last thirty years has revealed a core of such experiences that is found in very different cultures. A frequent element in this core is the 'being of light', a wonderful light that transforms anxiety into bliss and is also somehow a person. The person's identity differs according to the culture: for a Christian, for instance, the person may acquire the identity of Jesus. The light described by Plutarch is not a person, but in our passage of *Bacchae* it is twice identified with Dionysos.

Subsequently, Pentheus allows himself to be dressed in female clothes, as a maenad: this, in my view, reflects the gender-reversal characteristic of rites of passage. The effeminacy and transvestism of Dionysos is manifest in various texts from the fifth century BC (*Bacchae* 353; Aeschylus fragment 61) to the sixth century AD (Lydus *De Mensibus* 160) as well as in epithets and visual representations. It is – in part at least – a projection of the practice of transvestism in his ritual. He himself receives a garment from Rhea on being initiated into her mysteries (Apollodorus *Bibl.* 3.5.1).

This interpretation of *Bacchae* is confirmed by other evidence for Dionysiac mystery-cult. For instance, we will soon see in the Villa of the Mysteries at Pompeii another striking image of the anxiety of the Dionysiac initiand. The Christian writer Origen (*Against Celsus* 4.10) will mention apparitions and fearful things (*phasmata* and *deimata*) in Dionysiac initiation rituals. And the belief that dreaming about Dionysos signifies 'release from terrible things' (Artemidorus 2.37) surely drives from mystic initiation. When in *Bacchae* Pentheus says, on emerging from his house dressed as a maenad on his way to being dismembered, that he sees two suns and two cities of Thebes, this derives I believe from the widespread use of the *mirror* in the initial stage of Dionysiac mystery-cult to intrigue and confuse the initiand. Similarly, in a myth associated with mystic initiation, a mirror was used to lure Dionysos to dismemberment by the Titans. I have in my Commentary on *Bacchae* argued in detail for these and other such correspondences, which are too detailed and numerous to be coincidental.

It is virtually certain that in the lost part of Dionysos' speech at the end of the play he announced the establishment of his cult at Thebes. *Bacchae* dramatises the aetiological myth of the Theban cult of Dionysos, i.e. the myth that explains and narrates its founding. As such, it prefigures not only mystery-cult, the secrets of which are to be known only by the initiated, but also the festival that is open to all. Indeed Teiresias, as he goes to worship Dionysos on the mountainside, emphasises that the god requires honours from *everybody together*. This apparent contradiction does in fact correspond to a persistent feature of Dionysiac cult, the celebration of secret mystery-cult at the heart of a festival of the whole polis (see below).

In Aristophanes' *Frogs* (405 BC) the chorus of Eleusinian initiates enjoying themselves in the underworld deliver a proclamation of the kind delivered before mystic ritual, excluding from their choral dances anyone who has (357, cf. 368) 'not been initiated into the Bacchic rites of bull-eating Kratinos' (another comic dramatist). A recent interpretation of Aristophanes' *Frogs* (by Lada-Richards) brings to the understanding of Dionysos' trip to the underworld much light drawn from the Dionysiac mysteries. The *Frogs* is also among those texts that illustrate the role of Dionysos (as 'Iakchos)' in the mysteries at Eleusis.

Further invaluable evidence for Dionysiac initiation in this period is provided by the earliest of the so-called gold leaves, small inscribed strips of gold buried with the dead. The content of the inscriptions, although found in various parts of the Greek world, displays considerable overlap, and so indicates that they derive from the same matrix of ritual and belief. Almost certainly the ritual was Dionysiac mystic initiation. The use of a small quantity of gold does not mean that these initiates were very wealthy, but does at least rule out the possibility that Dionysiac initiation was always of the poorest. The dead initiates (male and female) take with them a record of what they learnt, in their initiatory rehearsal of death, about the underworld.

For instance, a gold leaf from Hipponion in southern Italy (c. 400 BC) gives instructions to the initiand about what to do in the underworld, including the instruction to go on the way trodden by other 'mystic initiates and *bakchoi*'. On another, from Thurii in southern Italy (early or mid-fourth century BC), are recorded ritual formulae which include the words 'Hail you who have suffered what you had never suffered before. You became a god instead of a mortal.' A gold leaf from Pelinna in Thessaly (one of a pair, late fourth century BC) contains the words

Now you died and now you came into being, thrice blessed one, on this day.

Tell Persephone that Bakchios himself freed you.

Bull, you jumped into milk.

Quickly you jumped into milk.

Ram, you fell into milk.

You have wine as your blessed honour (?).

And below the earth there await you the same rituals as the other blessed ones.

Whatever precisely is envisaged in these riddling formulae, it is of interest that the fundamental boundaries that separate mortals from deities on the one hand and animals on the other are dissolved, as they often are in Dionysiac cult. Such dissolution, along with the confusion of male with female and living with dead, is to be found especially in *Bacchae* (e.g. 4, 822, 857, 922). The idea of the unity of opposites is strikingly expressed also, we noted, on the mystic bone plates from Olbia. Its importance for the presocratic philosopher Herakleitos, as well as in Attic tragedy, also derives, I believe, at least in part from mystery-cult.

The wine mentioned in the Pelinna text may belong in the underworld, perhaps also in the ceremony itself, which seems to have prefigured the underworld. Attested elsewhere is the idea of wine-drinking by initiates in Hades (e.g. Plato *Republic* 363cd 'eternal drunkenness'). In Chapter 2 we saw that the invention of wine may have been in some way re-enacted in Dionysiac mystic initiation, as well as the importance of wine in depictions of what may be Dionysiac mystery-cult.

Another fourth-century indication of wine-drinking in mystic initiation is provided by an attack by Demosthenes (18.259–60) on his opponent Aeschines as assisting in various ways the initiations performed by his mother: reading the books, and by night performing various actions – putting fawnskins on the initiands, purifying them, smearing them with mud and bran, giving them drink from the mixing bowl, raising them up from the purification while telling them to say 'I escaped the bad, I found the better', priding himself on delivering the mightiest ever ululation (a kind of howl); and by day leading through the streets the fine thiasoi crowned with fennel and white poplar, squeezing the fat-cheeked snakes and raising them over his head, shouting 'Euoi Saboi' and dancing to the cry of 'Hyes Attes, Attes Hyes' (words of uncertain meaning), greeted by the old women as 'Leader and Instructor and Basket-bearer (*kistophoros*), Winnowing-basket-bearer (*liknophoros*)', and receiving as payment various kinds of cakes. With such rewards, concludes Demosthenes, who would not truly count himself and his fortunes blessed? The list of details is impressive, but has to be treated with caution, not least because the purpose of Demosthenes is ridicule.

Some of the details of this initiation suggest that it belonged to the Phrygian god Sabazios, others that it belonged to Dionysos. Perhaps it belonged to a synthesis of the two gods, facilitated by the association of both gods with Phrygia. In general the mystery-cults of different deities tend to interpenetrate, as a result of similarity of function (eternal blessedness) and structure. And so for example we have seen that the Pelinna text mentions Persephone (central to the mysteries of Eleusis) and Dionysos in the same line. Dionysos (as 'Iakchos') is important to the Eleusinian mysteries.

One of the Olbian bone plates mentioned above also contains the letters 'Orphic'. There is a tendency for mystery-cult to attribute to a mythical figure the invention of mystic rituals and the writing down of mystic wisdom. Such a mythical figure was 'Orpheus', who was asssociated with the Eleusinian mystery-cult, and was said to have founded Dionysiac mystery-cult, as well as 'Orphic' mystery-cult, which overlapped with the Dionysiac and took as its central myth the dismemberment of Dionysos at the hands of the Titans. In a fifth-century BC tragedy Theseus, irritated by what he thinks is the superior attitude of his son Hippolytus, sarcastically tells him 'with Orpheus as your lord be a *bakchos*, honouring the smoke of many writings' (Euripides *Hippolytus* 953–4); and in the next century Plato complains of purveyors of purifications and mystery-cults as producing 'a hubbub of books by Musaios and Orpheus' (*Republic* 364e).

In his *Phaedrus* Plato divides up divine madness into four kinds, each belonging to a god, assigns 'initiatory (*telestikē*)' madness to Dionysos (265), and in the same dialogue refers to initiations (*teletai*) in which release from suffering is provided for the person who 'is mad in the right way' (244e). I will return to this important passage in Chapter 8. Elsewhere Plato refers to 'purifications and initiations' involving the imitation of Nymphs, Pans, Silens, and Satyrs (*Laws* 815). And he often uses the language and structure of mystic initiation to express philosophical truth, notably in his *Symposium* and *Phaedrus*. This does not mean that he regards mystery-cult as itself the source of fundamental wisdom. Similarly Herakleitos of Ephesus, who is the first known philosopher (active circa 500 BC) to use terminology and ideas drawn from mystery-cult, condemns mystery-cult as actually practised, and is even reported to have threatened (among others) *mystai* ('initiates') and *bakchoi* with punishment after death (B14 D–K). The implication in Herakleitos and Plato may be that their wisdom is a truer or higher form of what is revealed in mystery-cult. As we shall see in Chapter 8, other intellectuals will adopt a similar position.

Still in the fourth-century BC, the mother of Alexander the Great, the Macedonian queen Olympias, performed Dionysiac cult in which tamed snakes slid out of mystic winnowing baskets (*likna*) – or so at least we are told centuries later by Plutarch (*Life of Alexander* 2). Moving on into the Hellenistic period, we find tableaux evoking Dionysiac mystery-cult in the grand procession held in Alexandria under king Ptolemy II Philadelphus , who reigned from 282 to 246 BC. And an inscription from Miletos of 276–5 BC embodies a contract for the sale of a priesthood of Dionysos to a woman who will preside over the public thiasos; but the inscription also permits any woman, if she wishes, to 'initiate to Dionysos' (i.e. to form a private thiasos) on payment to the public priestess of a regular fee.

Our next substantial evidence is provided by two papyri from the late third century BC, found in the sands of Egypt, which after its conquest by Alexander the Great in 332 BC had become a leading centre of Greek culture. One is a fragmentary papyrus, from the village of Gurôb, containing prescriptions for ritual. It includes the names of various deities, including Dionysos, and of objects (cone, bull-roarer, knucklebones, mirror) that we know from later texts to have been symbols used in Dionysos' mystery-cult. They seem here to be combined with elements from other mystery-cults, notably Sabazios' and the Eleusinian. In a poem (26) attributed to Theocritus (third century BC), sacred objects are in Dionysiac mystery-cult taken out of a basket (*kistē*) and placed on altars, but to be seen only by the initiated (26.8–9, 13–14).

The other significant papyrus from this period is the so-called Edict of Ptolemy IV Philopator (reigned 221–205 BC). It represents an extension of the centralised control of Dionysiac mysteries that we have seen at Miletos. Those 'initiating to Dionysos' in the countryside are required to sail to Alexandria in order to be registered. They are to make clear from whom they received the sacred objects (*hiera*) up to three generations back, and to deliver the sacred text (*hieros logos*) sealed and with the name of each initiator written on it. The mysteries seem to have been more an instrument of royal control than (as in *Bacchae*) an object of its hostility: there is evidence that Philopator took his own initiation seriously, and that he identified his regime with allegiance to Dionysos. It was his grandfather Ptolemy II Philadelphus who staged the procession with tableaux from Dionysiac mystery-cult. In the second century BC the monarchy of Pergamon will even put a symbol of the mysteries – a snake crawling out of a basket – on its widespread 'cistophoric' coinage.

ROMAN ITALY

When Rome expanded its power into southern Italy it incorporated a land that had long been – and continued to be – infused with Greek culture. This culture included Dionysiac mystery-cult. The consequent conflict, between Roman authority and the Greek cult of Dionysos, was no less dramatic than the fictional conflict between Dionysos and Pentheus in *Bacchae*.

The comic playwright Plautus (active from about 205 BC) alluded in several plays to the cult of Bacchus, for instance in his *Aulularia* (406–14), and in one instance to a verbal sign or password (*Miles Gloriosus* 1016) – suggesting secret understanding between mystic initiates. Shortly before the death of Plautus there occurred, in 186 BC, the suppression of Dionysiac associations in Italy by the Roman state, described in detail by Livy in the thirty-ninth book of his history of Rome. We also have an inscriptional version of the senatorial decree against the cult. Plautus in his *Casina* (a late play) wrote the words 'Now no Bacchic women are playing' (918) – conceivably a reference to the suppression.

Livy's account is derived from the official version of the episode, and so is suspect, for instance in its statement that the cult was involved in forging seals and wills (a typical accusation implying extreme untrustworthiness). But some of the practices he lists do correspond, albeit sometimes in a distorted way, with what – we know from other sources – was likely to have occurred in Dionysiac mystery-cult. For instance, the cult is said to have been originally confined to females, with males only admitted subsequently. Initiation includes making prayers in accordance with ritual formulae (*carmen sacrum*), with the priest dictating the words. This reminds us of the mystic formulae on the gold leaves, and of the dictation of a mystic formula described by Demosthenes (see above, p. 56).

The claims reported by Livy, that initiands were murdered (and their bodies never found), and that the cult was growing every day in popularity, are hardly consistent with each other. But the former claim may derive from the practice of inflicting on the initiand the terror of an *imagined* death, especially as in Livy's account the killing took the form of a *sacrifice*, as probably the imagined death of the Dionysiac initiand also frequently did. In *Bacchae*, Demosthenes, and Livy the mystery-cult is said to take place by *night*, a practice that aroused suspicion of sexual immorality in both Pentheus and the Roman authorities.

What was it about Dionysiac mystery-cult and the resulting associations that provoked massive (and apparently untypical) repression by the Roman state? Both Pentheus and the Roman senate feel threatened by what they regard as a new foreign cult (for Pentheus it is barbarian, for the Romans it is Greek). The god is called Liber (the Roman equivalent to, and name for, Dionysos) neither in Livy nor in the senatorial decree, and this confirms that he was felt as alien.

But in fact Dionysiac mystery-cult was not as new to Italy as Livy suggests. It had been present in Greek areas of southern Italy as early as the fifth and fourth centuries BC, and evidence for it in Rome is provided by graves of the third century BC. Probably an important factor for the Roman authorities was growth in the popularity of the cult, to which the contemporary flourishing of the Dionysiac mysteries in the eastern Mediteranean may have contributed.

The cult combined relatively sophisticated organisation (including of economic resources) with secrecy, and with *individual choice* to be initiated (rather than adherence dictated by locality, family, patronage, tradition, authority, and so on), all of which was outside the control of the political authorities. According to Livy it was felt to constitute 'almost a second people (or 'alternative society': *alterum . . . populum*)' and a 'conspiracy' (*coniuratio*) aiming to control the state. Individual choice seems to have been from the earliest evidence for mystery-cult a feature that distinguished it from many other rituals. It is interesting that a female associate of Spartacus in the slave revolt of 73 BC was said to have prophesied about him while she was 'possessed by Dionysiac rituals' (Plutarch *Life of Crassus* 8.4).

Moreover, in Dionysos – and especially in his mystery-cult – we have seen a tendency to *destroy boundaries*. The Roman authorities deplored the mingling of males and females in the cult, and indeed the effeminacy of male initiates. And the cult may have mingled adherents from very different social classes, thereby seeming to challenge the class structure of the Roman state. In *Bacchae* Dionysos is said to insist on having worship from everybody, without distinctions, and he himself is effeminate. The intensity of the cult, together with the secret initiation and oath of loyalty to which its members were subjected, may have been – or seemed to be – a focus of identity that transcended, and so threatened loyalty to, the existing structures of the Roman order. Young initiates were, it is claimed, unlikely to be good soldiers.

The suppression was no doubt confined to what were seen as politically threatening forms of the cult. Restricted forms were allowed to continue. Moreover, the rise of populist leaders may have created circumstances more favourable to the god. Marius (c. 157–86 BC), who made recruitment into the army more inclusive and was the first of a new kind of politician who dominated Rome by the following arising from military success, was said to have used a special kind of drinking-cup (the *kantharos*) after the example of Liber (Val. Max. 3.6.6). Another such leader, a generation later, was Julius Caesar (100–44 BC), who is believed by some scholars to have aspired to kingship of the Hellenistic type, and was even rumoured to want to transfer the capital of the Roman empire to Alexandria (Sueton *Div. Jul.* 79; Nik. Damask. 20), a centre of Dionysiac cult where he had spent much time with the queen of Egypt, Kleopatra. A much later report (Servius on Virgil *Eclogues.* 5.29) called it undisputed that Caesar was the first to introduce the cult (*sacra*) of Liber into Rome. This cannot as it stands be true, but it may reflect an interest of Caesar's in reviving or formalising the cult of the god, with or without mystery-cult.

It was at any rate during the rise to power of Caesar that there was painted the most striking surviving visual representation of mystic initiation – in the Villa Item or 'Villa of the Mysteries' at Pompeii. This fresco was painted around the walls of a small room in a private house whose large size is clear evidence for the adherence of the wealthy to mystery-cult. Because every scene in it has been the subject of controversy, and a definitive account is impossible, I will be brief. At the centre of the composition is the figure of Dionysos seated and lolling in the lap of a female who is either his mother Semele or (more likely) his lover Ariadne. Next to them is a female in the act of removing a veil from a phallus in a *liknon*. The *liknon* is a winnowing basket that appears in other evidence (textual and visual) for Dionysiac mystery-cult. Next to it there stands a female figure with dark wings and high boots, who is making a gesture of aversion towards the *liknon* with her left hand and with her right hand is flagellating – across the corner of the room – a kneeling, semi-naked female figure who has her eyes closed (as an initiand, no doubt) and her head in the lap of another

Figure 4 Friezes from the Villa of the Mysteries, Pompeii.

Source: Photo © 1997 Margaret M. Curran. Reproduced by permission of Leo Curran.

(seated) female. It is to this wretched female, it seems, that the phallus is about to be revealed (Figure 4).

There is some evidence for the practice of flagellation as a (purificatory?) ordeal in mystic initiation. Here the practice is, it seems, imagined as allegorical. Who is the (allegorical) winged female? There have been numerous suggestions, and certainty is impossible. My preferred candidate is Ignorance, a suggestion supported in particular by a mural from Hadrianic Egypt of Oedipus being impelled by a (labelled) female personification of ignorance (in the same bodily posture as our winged female, but without rod and wings) to kill his father, as well as by a passage of Achilles Tatius' *Cleitophon and Leucippe* (5.23.6) in which the narrator describes the experience of being beaten: 'as in mystery-cult, I knew nothing'. A precondition for the effectiveness of mystic initiation is initial agonising ignorance of its blissful outcome (a reason why the cult has to be secret). With the transition from ignorance to knowledge (at the unveiling of the phallus), Ignorance, who has caused the anxiety, must suddenly fly off. In other visual representations of the unveiling of the *liknon* or Silenos-mask a winged female, making the same gesture of aversion towards the unveiling with her left hand, is actually moving away from it.

Next to the flagellated female is a dancing maenad (perhaps representing the joy that followed the agonising ignorance), and beyond her a bride being adorned, and then, on the adjacent wall, a mature seated female who seems to look back calmly across the room at the scene of flagellation.

On the other side of Dionysos is a group of four figures: a seated Silenos holding up a cup into which there peers a young male with pointed ears (presumably a satyr), and behind him another young satyr holding up a fierce Silenos-mask. Across the corner is a female moving away in terror, apparently at something occurring in the group of three male figures. What is occurring there? Some scholars think it is lecanomancy (divining by an image in liquid in the cup), others catoptromancy (divining by a reflection – perhaps of the fierce mask – on the metallic surface of the cup). If the young satyr is looking at a reflection, then there may be a connection with the use of the mirror in Dionysiac mystic initiation.

Next to the terrified woman there is an idyllic scene comprising male and female mythical followers of Dionysos, and beyond them there are scenes of ritual (notably a child reading from a text, and purification) performed by mortals and probably painted as preliminary to the terrors of the initiation itself. The child reading reminds us of Aeschines assisting his mother by reading, and of the sacred texts mentioned in the Edict of Ptolemy IV Philopator.

To summarise the whole sequence: there is an inner group of the god with lover (or mother), then on either side figures of myth, and then, beyond them on either side, the mortals who by their participation in the ritual enter the realm of myth and of deity.

THE ROMAN EMPIRE

Just as *Bacchae* is the richest literary source for Dionysiac mystery-cult, so the Villa of the Mysteries is the richest visual source. Thereafter there are numerous pieces of evidence (visual, literary, and inscriptional), but each of them by itself tells us very little about the heart of the ritual. I will mention some of these pieces, starting with the visual.

Various works of art, mostly from Roman Italy of the imperial period (i.e. from 31 BC onwards), show scenes of Dionysiac initiation. Perhaps the most explicit, albeit somewhat damaged, are some stucco reliefs from the 'Villa Farnesina', a lavish villa of the reign of Augustus (31 BC–14 AD). Better preserved are the terracotta plaques known as 'Campana reliefs' (mid-first century BC to mid-second century AD), some of which show elements of Dionysiac mystery-cult. So do also various kinds of artefact, notably cups made in the workshop of Marcus Perennius at Arezzo (of the Augustan period), as well as mosaics, and sarcophagi with sculpted reliefs, from various parts of the Roman empire from the first to the fourth centuries AD.

Of these representations three general features deserve emphasis. The first is the frequent appearance of the *liknon* containing sacred objects (notably the phallus) to be revealed to the initiand, as we saw in the Villa of the Mysteries. The second is the presence of mythical followers of Dionysos, notably Silenos: this suggests that the ritual included dressing up in mythical roles, an impression strengthened by the frequent presence of *masks*. Again, the Villa of the Mysteries shows us more than one Satyr, as well as a mask of Silenos. Third, in several of the representations the initiands are *children*.

This is not say that all these scenes focus on a Dionysiac initiation as elaborately as the Villa of the Mysteries fresco seems to do. Consider, for example, the sarcophagi. It was mystery-cult that underlay the frequent association of Dionysos with death that is to be found throughout antiquity from Homer onwards (Chapter 6). A large proportion of the sarcophagi have scenes of Dionysiac well-being: groups of figures, some of them identifiable as mythical figures such as Ariadne or Silenos, engaging in ecstatic dance, alcoholic revelry, the vintage, the triumphal procession of Dionysos, erotic activity, and so on. Given that they were sculpted on sarcophagi, these scenes must have been associated with the well-being of the dead, and contrast in their unrestrained sensuality with the sobriety of most Christian funerary art. This association of Dionysiac scenes with the next world is confirmed by the presence, in some of the scenes, of images (notably the initiand with covered head, and the *liknon* containing the veiled phallus) that do not form a complete or detailed scene of initiation but do nevertheless evoke the mystic ritual process by which Dionysiac well-being in the next world is obtained.

It may be difficult to determine, in a Dionysiac work of art, the extent to which the images cohere by evoking the next world indicated in mystic initiation. For instance, a mosaic in a villa discovered in Cologne, of the early third century AD, represents Dionysos, satyrs, maenads, a shepherd, Pan, eroticism, music and dance, shells, a fig-tree, *likna*, fruit, drinking vessels, grapes, a panther, a lion, an ass, a goat, a fox, baskets of fruit, flowers, doves, ducks, parrots, guinea-fowl, and peacocks. It is possible to see most of these images as appropriate decoration for a dining room. But it has also been argued that everything in the mosaic has a specific meaning in a Dionysiac context, in particular as evoking something of the happy hereafter created by Dionysiac mystic ritual. Even the parrot, for example, is depicted elsewhere frequently along with grapes (for instance in a funerary chamber), and in a room (unearthed in Pergamon) that may have been sacred to Dionysos. The parrot had been brought from India, from which Dionysos returned in triumph, and was carried in the Dionysiac procession of Ptolemy II Philadelphus. It was Dionysiac in its taste for wine and its fascination with its own image in a mirror (compare Chapter 8). And its apparent capacity for human speech transcends the boundary between human and animal, and so makes it one of the creatures attracted by the singing of Orpheus.

The same possibility – that apparently decorative details may in fact be given coherence by their association with Dionysiac mystery-cult – attaches to the narrative *Daphnis and Chloe* by Longus, roughly contemporary with the Cologne mosaic. It narrates the developing love of two foundlings brought up by shepherds on the island of Lesbos. It has been argued, somewhat controversially, that the narrative corresponds in detail to the mystery-cult of the god. And so for instance the suckling (at the beginning of the story) of Daphnis by a goat and of Chloe by a sheep, and (at the end) of their son by a goat and of their daughter by a sheep, may derive from, and evoke, an element of mystic initiation. The infant Dionysos was suckled by a goat, and in one version by a maenad named 'goat' (*Eriphe*). On a tomb roughly contemporary with Longus he is being suckled by a goat next to the *cista mystica* containing a snake (i.e. in the context of mystic ritual). On one of the gold leaves containing formulae uttered in Dionysiac mystic initiation there is the puzzling formula 'A kid (*eriphos*) I fell into milk'. Conversely, but no less expressive of the unity of humankind with nature, in Euripides' *Bacchae* (700) the maenads suckle a roe or wolf-cubs, and in the idyllic scene in the initiation ritual painted in the Pompeian Villa of the Mysteries a young woman with pointed ears suckles a kid.

Whether or not we assent to every detail of the mystic interpretation of mosaic and narrative, undoubtedly they will appear differently (for instance less arbitrary) to those who have acquired knowledge of the cult and mysteries of Dionysos. These mysteries seem, in the imperial period, to imply hope for well-being in the hereafter grounded in the cycle of generation in nature – an idea not found in the classical period (e.g. in the gold leaves of the fourth century BC).

A special category of evidence for the mysteries in the Roman empire, and for the associations that practised them, consists of *inscriptions*. We possess about two hundred, almost all in Greek, found in various parts of the Roman empire (especially in Asia Minor), from the third century BC to the fourth century AD, though mostly from the first three centuries AD. Because there is no co-ordinating centre for the associations, it is unsurprising that there is very little homogeneity among them. The inscriptions frequently mention 'mystic initiates' (*mustai*) or 'fellow mystic initiates' (*sunmustai, summustai*) and in a few cases a 'revealer of the sacred' (*hierophantēs*); and sometimes they indicate a role for the association in the performance of public rituals (such as the *Katagōgia*, the escort of Dionysos into the city). In these respects the associations resemble the first detailed picture of a Dionysiac association – albeit one imagined in myth – from Euripides' *Bacchae*. But in other respects they could hardly be more different. In *Bacchae* the ecstatic dancing by the Theban women on the mountainside coheres with the Asiatic chorus' characterisation of initiation as 'joining the soul to the thiasos', and comes into violent conflict with political authority. But the associations recorded centuries later by the inscriptions often contain both sexes, are all-male more commonly than all-female, tend to be controlled by males rather than by females, are hierarchical rather than (as in *Bacchae*) egalitarian, and are much concerned with administrative, financial, and disciplinary detail. Some of them have their own cult places, and some are thoroughly integrated into the structure of political power – sometimes even honouring the Roman emperor. An inscription (188: numbers are from the collection by Jaccottet) from Latium (circa 165 AD), consisting of over 400 names in about 25 categories such as priests, *boukoloi* (cowherds), *liknāphoroi* (*liknon*-bearers), and *antrophulakes* (cave guardians), seems to be pervaded by the hierarchy of Roman society and unified by dependence on a powerful *familia*.

Given the occurrence in the inscriptions *of* the words *teletē*, and *orgia*, referring to mystic ritual, as well as *mustēs* and *hierophantēs*, it is likely that in general the associations performed initiatory ritual. Occasionally we find evidence of consciousness of such ritual as an ancient tradition, for instance in the performance of an 'ancient *teletē*' at Tomis on the Black Sea. However – and in contrast to attacks by Christian writers and to visual representations – very little of initiatory ritual is revealed by the inscriptions, which, as public documents, cannot be expected to reveal what has to be secret. Just as Dionysos in *Bacchae* told Pentheus that the mysteries, though worth knowing, cannot be spoken to the uninitiated (472–4), so an inscription at Halikarnoss of the second or first century BC enjoins on the initiate knowledge of how to be silent about what is secret and to speak what is permitted.

The celebrations that the inscriptions do indicate are very various, and it is often difficult to tell whether they belong to initiation ritual or to the repeated celebrations of the whole initiated group. If the Dionysiac association of Callatis (on the west coast of the Black Sea) used their (apparently tomb-like) 'cave' to simulate the underworld, then it may well have been used to subject initiands to an experience of death (54–61). And a few inscriptions indicate the carrying of the *liknon*, which is common in contemporary visual representations of Dionysiac initiation. But there are also practices which, though conceivably part of an initiatory festival, seem more likely to be no more than celebrations by the whole association. We read of sacrifice and feasting on certain days of the year, and, in a few inscriptions, of hymns and dances.

We may even infer the performance of dramas. In an inscription from Magnesia-on-the-Maiander (147) of the beginning of the second century AD certain *mustai*, male and female, have the title 'nurse of Dionysos' or 'nurse', suggesting either the performance of a drama about the infancy of the god or at least dressing in costumes of the Nymphs or Silens who were his nurses. The especially detailed Athenian inscription (of the third quarter of the second century AD) of an all-male association calling itself the *Iobakchoi* (4) records – along with rules for admission and for discipline at feasts – the requirement 'with all good order and calm to speak and perform the parts (*merismous*) under the direction of the *archibakchos*'. Further, the *archibakchos* is to perform a sacrifice and libation on the tenth day of the month Elaphebolion (the first day of the City Dionysia, at which drama was performed), and after the dividing up of the victim, the priest, the deputy priest, the *archibakchos*, the treasurer, the *boukolikos*, Dionysos, Korē, Palaemon, Aphrodite, and Prōteurythmos are each to take (their piece of meat). The remains have survived of the building in which this association met, as have also the walls (once decorated with Dionysiac paintings), benches, and altars of the Dionysiac association of 'cowherds' (*boukoloi*) at Pergamon. At Smyrna we hear, in several inscriptions of the first and second centuries AD, of an association that is in one of them called 'the assembly of *technitai* (i.e. actors) and *mustai* around Dionysos Breiseus' (121).

A few other inscriptions also seem to indicate the impersonation of satyrs and silens, as do numerous visual representations (such as the Villa of the Mysteries frieze). For instance, an initiate honoured by an inscription (113) from Philadelphia in Lydia (second century AD) is represented as a dancing satyr. The urban associations adopt rural symbolism. We hear of *stibades* (couches made of vegetation) and caves. A common title found in the inscriptions is *boukolos*, cowherd.

It has been maintained that these associations did not possess the kind of serious religious feeling that we find in Dionysiac cult of an earlier age, even that the main point was a rural outing for town-dwellers. Such celebrations may well have been more important to the group than was the creation of new members by initiation. But the cult may have had more emotional intensity than appears: the inscriptions, after all, have limited purposes (good order within the group, financial arrangements, honouring benefactors, etc.) and cannot be expected to reveal all. We have seen that the performance of drama, or at least the ritual enactment of myth, may in fact belong to mystic initiation. The reference, in a third century AD inscription from Rhodes (159), to a water-organist awakening the god may suggest a ritual in which the experience of the initiate returning from death is modelled on the awakening of Dionysos. In an epitaph from southeast Bulgaria (45) the dead woman is said to have been honoured by the *lusiponos* ('releaser from pain', probably Dionysos but perhaps Zeus) 'like Semele'. This indicates perhaps a mystic ritual in which the woman was imagined to participate in the death and apotheosis of Semele, a myth which – like the 'nurses' at Magnesia-on-the-Maiander and numerous visual representations of Dionysiac mystic ritual – involves the childhood of Dionysos.

In a Latin inscription from near Philippi (29), seemingly of the third century AD, a dead boy is imagined as being welcomed, as a satyr, in a flowery meadow by female initiates marked with the sign of Bromios (Dionysos) or by Naiads bearing mystic baskets. Here it seems that the impersonation of immortal beings (nymphs and satyrs) by the initiates is imagined as continuing into the rural setting of the next world. In the same period the Bulgarian epitaph we have just referred to (45) imagines a priestess as being lamented by satyrs.

The next world is imagined in terms of the rituals or celebrations performed in this. A *mustēs* in Macedonia (second century AD) is said to have escaped to the vines of Hades (23). A young man buried in Lydia in the third century AD is imagined as claimed by Dionysos to be his companion in choral dances (112). And the epitaph (180) of a young girl in Tusculum (second century AD?) imagines Dionysos making her leader of the *speira* in the choral dance (*speira* was a word used for Dionysiac associations). In *Bacchae* Dionysos associates establishing his initiation rituals at Thebes with making people dance (*Bacchae* 21–2). And centuries later Lucian writes that there is no ancient mystic initiation without dancing (*On Dance* 15). According to Plutarch people believe that by being purified in mystic rituals they will 'continue playing and dancing in Hades' (*Moralia* 1105). In Aristophanes' *Frogs* the Eleusinian initiates in the underworld invite Iakchos (the Eleusinian Dionysos) to take part in their dances in the meadows.

As for the relation of dancing to the mystic transition from anxiety to joy, a clue is given by the fragment of Plutarch mentioned above (p. 53), in which he says that the experience of the soul on the point of death is like being initiated into the great mysteries, that after various kinds of anxiety and suffering there is a wonderful light, meadows, and (among other delights) dancing. Perhaps the culmination of the ritual, the entry into eternal bliss, was marked by the initiates coming together in a dance that contrasted with the anxious and chaotic movements of each isolated individual that seem to have characterised the earlier phase of the ritual transition. But dance was not necessarily restricted to this phase (at Eleusis it occurred in various phases of the festival).

Finally, some light on the celebrations of the Dionysiac association may be shed by a surviving collection of eighty-seven anonymous 'Orphic Hymns', composed to be used by a band of initiates some-where in western Asia Minor. It is of unknown date, but could easily have been composed in the second century AD. Of the numerous gods mentioned, Dionysos is especially prominent. One hymn (44) speaks of Semele's birth-pain for her son Dionysos being re-enacted every other year along with 'pure mysteries'. Another (77) asks the goddess Memory to arouse in the initiates memory of the sacred initiation ritual, sending away from them forgetfulness. In general these hymns ask for well-being in *this* world.

FESTIVAL AND MYSTERY

Plato (*Republic* 364b–e) maintains that certain seers and itinerant priests manage to persuade 'not only private individuals but also cities (*poleis*)' that there are liberations (*luseis*), purifications, and *teletai* (mystic rituals) to free us from sufferings in the next world. One such priest was the legendary Melampous, who according to Herodotus introduced Dionysiac cult into Greece (from Egypt), and by curing the Argive women of madness obtained for himself and his brother most of the kingdom of Argos (2.49; 9.34). Dionysos himself in *Bacchae* comes to Thebes disguised as an itinerant priest, and announces that it is the polis that has to learn his mystery-cult (39–40). Mystery-cult is on the one hand practised secretly, by a small group, but on the other hand may belong to the official calendar of the polis. This duality was a factor in the genesis of tragedy (Chapter 7).

A feature of Dionysiac cult that we have noted more than once is the celebration of secret cult within a public festival of the whole community. For instance, at the Athenian Lenaia festival, there seems to have been mystic ritual of some kind. At the Athenian Anthesteria festival sacred objects were handled and secret ritual performed 'on behalf of the city' (according to the fourth-century BC speech *Against Neaira*) by a band of fourteen women. A distinction of this kind may lie behind a saying recorded as 'about the mystic initiations' by Plato (*Phaedo* 69c): 'many are fennel-carriers, but few are *bakchoï*'. ('Fennel' here refers to the *thrysos*, a fennel-rod crowned with ivy, often carried in Dionysiac cult.)

Moving on four centuries we find Plutarch (Moralia 293d) describing the Delphic festival *Herois* as having 'for the most part a mystic account (*mustikos logos*), which the Thyiades [maenads] know, but from what is done openly one would imagine a bringing up of Semele'. In the same period Pausanias (2.7.5–6) reports that at a temple of Dionysos near the theatre of Sikyon there are images of the god and of maenads. The Sikyonians also have some images in a concealed place (*en aporrhētōi*), which on one night of the year they carry to the temple with torchlight and local hymns. One of the images is named *Bakcheios*, and is followed by the other, named *Lusios* (Liberator), once brought from Thebes by 'Phanes' (another example of an individual causing a city to adopt liberating mystic ritual, as described by Plato). At another city, Bryseai in Laconia, there is according to Pausanias a temple of Dionysos containing an image of the god, and another image of him in the open (3.20.3). Only women may see the image within, because it is women who by themselves perform the sacrifices in secret (*en aporrhētōi*).

In both Sikyon and Bryseai there survives an ancient tradition, such as we described earlier, of mystic ritual as the concealed part of a manifestation of the polis as a whole (festival, temple). The words *Lusios* (of Dionysos) and *aporrhētos* strongly suggest mystery-cult. Compare for example Dionysos *liberating* the initiand on the Pelinna gold leaf quoted above (p. 55). The two images of Dionysos at Sikyon seem to express two aspects of initiation, frenzy (*bakcheia*) and liberation. 'Phanes' was also the name of a creator deity in Orphic cosmology, and may be taken to mean 'revealer' or 'illuminator' – in this context by torchlight, for according to an ancient text (*Rhesus* 943) 'Orpheus made known the torches (*phanai*) of secret (*aporrhētōn*) mysteries.'

An even later instance of this duality – secret ritual and public festival – is provided by a passage (*Ep.* 17.4) of Augustine (354–430 AD) written in response to the criticism that Christians – in contrast to traditional religion – are exclusive and see their god in secret places. Augustine points out that the critic has forgotten Liber (Dionysos), who is shown only to a few initiated, and then berates him with the public aspect of the same cult as consisting of prominent citizens going in a bacchic frenzy through the streets.

RITUAL, MYTH, AND THE NEXT WORLD

Rituals in the ancient world are generally associated with myths. The myth, as a projection of the ritual, may explain its origin, justify it, or give it meaning. For instance, the Eleusinian mysteries were associated with the myth of Demeter losing her daughter Korē to Hades, as narrated in the *Homeric Hymn to Demeter*. Dionysiac mystic initiation is projected in the experiences of Pentheus in *Bacchae*. One of his experiences is to be dismembered, and have his dismembered body reconstituted by his mother. Dismemberment is not uncommon, in initiation rituals of various cultures, as an imagined ordeal of the initiand. But one would expect it to be followed by restoration to wholeness and life. Pentheus is restored by his mother to wholeness, but – being a mortal – cannot be restored to life. Dionysos, on the other hand, after being dismembered by the Titans, *is* restored (in one version by his mother: Diodorus 3.62.6) to life as well as to wholeness.

Pentheus and Dionysos are both frenzied, and both combine male with female and human with animal, because they are both (in part) projections of the mystic initiand. But just as mystic initiation embodies the opposed aspects of resistance (to the transition) and death, on the one hand, and on the other the achievement of immortality (through the transition), so Pentheus embodies the former aspect and Dionysos the latter. Dionysos could be called 'Initiate' (*Mustēs*: Pausanias 8.54.5), and even shares the name *bakchos* with his initiates (e.g. *Bacchae* 491, 623), but his successful transition to immortality – his restoration to life and his circulation between the next world and this one – allows him also to be their divine saviour.

Moreover, in order that initiands should experience the necessary preliminary fear, the public myth of Pentheus embodies an *irreversible* death. The dismemberment and restoration to life of Dionysos, on the other hand, seems to have been for some time kept out of the public domain, so that some scholars have denied its existence before the first certain reference to it in the third century BC (Callimachus fragment 643). But there are several earlier passages that seem to allude to it (Chapter 8). And in the second century AD Pausanias (8.37.5) reports – albeit perhaps unreliably – that Onomacritus, who we know to have been active in sixth-century Athens, 'composed *orgia* (mystery-cult) for Dionysos and made the Titans the agents of his sufferings'.

Eventually the myth seems to have lost its secrecy. Diodorus, a contemporary of Julius Caesar, tells us (3.62.8) that the things that are revealed in the Orphic poems and introduced into initiation rituals agree with the myth of the dismemberment of Dionysos by the Titans and of the restoration of his limbs to their natural state. Plutarch (*Moralia* 364) compares Dionysos to the Egyptian Osiris, stating that 'the story about the Titans and the Night-festivals agree with what is related of Osiris – dismemberments and returns to life and rebirths'. In another passage (389a) he mentions various transformations undergone by Dionysos, and that 'the cleverer people . . . construct certain destructions and disappearances, followed by returns to life and rebirths, riddles and myths in keeping with the aforesaid transformations'. The restoration of Dionysos to life was (like the return of Korē from Hades at Eleusis) presumably connected with the immortality obtained by the initiates.

Clement of Alexandria (*Protrepticus* 2.18) mentions the toys by which the Titans lured Dionysos to his dismemberment, and explicitly associates them with various symbolic objects (*symbola*) used in the mystic ritual: knucklebone, ball, spinning-top (or cone), apples, bull-roarer, mirror, fleece. Four of these objects appeared in the late third-century BC fragmentary papyrus from Gurôb mentioned earlier in this chapter (p. 58). Plutarch consoles his wife with the immortality promised by 'the mystic *symbol* – of which we who are participants share knowledge – of the Dionysiac rites' (611d). And Apuleius refers to his careful conservation of signs and monuments (*signa et monumenta*) handed to him by priests in initiations, and adds that those of his audience who are initiates of Liber Pater (the ancient Italian god identified with Dionysos) know what they have concealed at home and venerate in silence away from all profane people (*Apology* 55). He also calls them *crepundia*, toys, and so they are presumably the toys which various texts say were used by the Titans to lure Dionysos to his dismemberment.

How did the performance of the mystic ritual relate to mythical dismemberment? Unreliable is the scholiast on Clement *Protrepticus* 12.119: 'those being initiated to Dionysos ate raw meat to indicate the tearing apart of Dionysos by the Maenads'. And there is no evidence that Dionysiac initiands were imagined as undergoing (like Dionysos) *bodily* restoration. There is a contrast here with the Christian hope, based on the resurrection of Jesus, for bodily resurrection (the relationship between the two cults deserves investigation, which it will receive in Chapter 9). Mystic initiation generally ensures happiness for initiates in the next world, which may (given the destruction of the mortal body) be for the immortal *soul*. I will suggest in Chapter 8 that the bodily fragmentation of Dionysos (and his restoration to wholeness) was a model for the *psychic* fragmentation (and restoration to wholeness) of the initiand.

Not inconsistent with this is the possibility that the dismemberment myth was related to the drinking of wine that we have seen to be common in the mystic ritual. The myth was interpreted as signifying the creation of wine out of the crushed grapes (Diodorus 3.62), and wine is earlier identified with Dionysos himself (e.g. *Bacchae* 284), more specifically with his blood (Timotheos fragment 780). Conceivably psychic wholeness induced by wine was associated with the restoration to wholeness of Dionysos dismembered in the making of the wine.

Religious ritual, and indeed religion in general, attempts to control the power of what is unknown. The unknown power that mystic initiation attempts to control is the power of death. And so it pre-enacts, in the controlled form of ritual, the process of dying. It stages the anxiety of death that leads to the bliss of the next world. And so because death is an unpredictable rupture of personal identity, mystic initiation must abolish the fundamental categories that constitute personal identity. It may therefore, as we have seen, enact a controlled confusion of male with female, human with animal, living with dead, mortal with immortal. And because the power of death is absolute, the even greater power that is bestowed by control over it easily becomes a political issue. And so mystery-cult may, as we have seen, conflict with political authority and with the political ambitions of Christianity, and finally yields to the latter.

OVERVIEW

After in the first section delineating the main features of mystery-cult, in the next two sections we followed the most important evidence for Dionysiac mystery-cult thoughout Graeco-Roman antiquity. It is perhaps not a coincidence that the two most important pieces of evidence, one from classical Athens and the other from first-century BC Italy, are also among the most striking *aesthetic* achievements of the ancient world: Euripides' *Bacchae* and the Villa Item frieze. The remaining sections concerned the relationship of mystery-cult to the public festival, leading into Chapter 7, and to conceptions of death and dismemberment, leading into Chapters 6, 8, and 9.

6

DEATH

INTRODUCTION: MYSTERY-CULT AND DEATH

It is only to be expected that a deity so associated with the vigorous life of nature (Chapter 2) should also have a function in the face of death. But in fact most of the forms of association between Dionysos and death are derived, directly or indirectly, from the attempt by humans to control their experience of death, in mystery-cult.

And so we must from the beginning be clear about the three ways in which Dionysos' association with death derives from mystery-cult. First, the dismemberment of his enemy Pentheus expresses not just the futility of resistance to the god but also the idea of the death of the initiand (Chapter 5). The idea of Dionysos as a savage killer, for instance as 'Man-shatterer' (*anthrōporraistēs*) on the island of Tenedos, probably derives, at least in part, from this function in mystery-cult. Second, a secret of the mystery-cult was that dismemberment is in fact to be followed by restoration to life, and this transition was projected onto the immortal Dionysos, who is accordingly in the myth himself dismembered and then restored to life. Third, this power of Dionysos over death, his positive role in the ritual, makes him into a saviour of his initiates in the next world.

EARLY EVIDENCE

This is not to say that Dionysos' association with death in myth is always directly connected with mystery-cult. The earliest surviving

Dionysiac myth is in Homer: Ariadne is killed by Artemis 'on the testimony of Dionysos' (*Odyssey* 11.325). The story of Ariadne being united with Dionysos (and immortalised) after being abandoned by Theseus is well known (e.g. Figure 7). But there seems to have been a rare version of the myth in which Ariadne left Dionysos for Theseus: perhaps the participation of Dionysos in her death derives (as punishment) from this version. But it may in fact (also?) derive – albeit indirectly – from mystery-cult, expressing a deep structure in which Dionysos imposes death as a preliminary to immortality.

Of the four brief mentions of Dionysos in Homer, there are in fact two in which he is associated with death. The other is *Odyssey* 24.74: it was Dionysos who gave to Thetis the golden amphora (*amphiphoreus*, generally used to contain wine) that subsequently contained – in wine and oil – the bones of her son Achilles mixed with those of Patroklos.

The passage of this same golden amphora from gift of Dionysos to funerary container was described by the sixth century BC poet Stesichorus (234 *PMG*), and it has even been speculatively identified with the amphora carried by Dionysos as a wedding gift for Achilles' parents on the François Vase (Chapter 2): if so, this would prefigure the frequent interpenetration of death ritual and wedding in the Dionysiac genre of Athenian tragedy. The ashes of the dead were often placed in vessels, and these vessels might often be of the kind to contain wine. This is not the only association of wine with death ritual, for it might be used also in libations or to wash the body.

In one lost play (*Sisyphos*) by Aeschylus the ruler of the underworld, Plouton, was called Zagreus, in another (*Aigyptioi*) Zagreus was the son of Hades, and in later texts Zagreus was frequently identified with Dionysos. More explicit is the statement of Aeschylus' contemporary Herakleitos that

> were it not for Dionysos that they were making the procession and singing the song to the genitals [i.e. the phallic hymn], they would be acting most shamefully. But Hades is the same as Dionysos, for whom they rave and perform the Lenaia (B15 D–K).

The obscenity at the Dionysiac festival would be shameful without its deeper meaning, namely the unity of the opposites of death and (phallic?) generation in the mystery-cult that is often at the heart of the festival (Chapter 5). Herakleitos' doctrine of the (concealed but fundamental) unity of opposites derives – in part at least – from mystery-cult, notably from the unity of death and life implicit in the mystic transition. Here the doctrine seems reinforced by the similarity of the terms used (in the Greek 'without shame' is *an-aides*, 'Hades' is *Aides*).

DIONYSOS IN THE UNDERWORLD

The identification of Hades with Dionysos is Herakleitos' epigrammatic formulation of a cultic reality. But although there are some visual manifestations of this identification (or confusion) in the classical period, easier to be sure of is Dionysos' frequent *association* with underworld deities. For instance, on some of the dedicated terracotta plaques (*pinakes*) from Lokri in southern Italy Dionysos appears before the enthroned Persephone, queen of the underworld, or before her and Hades enthroned together.

These plaques are generally dated from 480 to 440 BC. Shortly thereafter in southern Italy and Sicily began the production, that continued to the end of the fourth century BC, of the numerous red-figured vases that have been discovered in tombs. Given the sepulchral destination of these vases, it is unsurprising to find on them a fair amount of eschatological imagery (i.e. about the next world). They may even have been used in the funeral ceremony for the libation or consumption of wine. The deity who appears most frequently on them is Dionysos. Also common are his companions (satyrs and maenads), and Dionysiac equipment such as the thyrsos, as well as the mirror (an object used in the Dionysiac mysteries: Chapter 5). When for instance such Dionysiac scenes are located in a meadow, or the dead person is equipped with accoutrements of the thiasos, then surely we have what is imagined to await the initiated in the next world. An example of this kind of Dionysiac idyll is described in the next chapter, as it occurs on the same vase as a picture (also of probable eschatological significance) inspired by *tragedy*. Vases are not however the only Dionysiac items to be buried with the dead. Still in southern Italy, we might mention a statuette of a dancing maenad found clasped in the hand of a young woman buried at Lokri about 400 BC.

There were specific burial customs 'known as Orphic and Bacchic' (Herodotus 2.81), and a fifth-century BC inscription from Cumae forbids burial to all save Dionysiac initiates. Some objects found in tombs identify the dead as initiated, notably the funerary gold leaves inscribed with mystic formulae, and a mirror inscribed with the Dionysiac cry *euai* (circa 500 BC) from Olbia north of the Black sea. Nevertheless, probably at least some Dionysiac symbols were well enough known to accompany even the uninitiated to the next world. This is even more likely much later, in the imperial period, with images of the Dionysiac thiasos and its symbols regularly decorating the tombs of those who could afford it. In the imperial period there are also sepulchral images that identify the dead person with Dionysos (as in Apuleius *Metamorphoses* 8.7), but even this does not necessarily imply mystic initiation. Not did mystic initiation ever necessarily exclude the need for intense lamentation.

On an Apulian *krater* (mixing-bowl) dated 335–325 BC (now in Toledo, Ohio) there is painted on one side a tomb and its occupant, and on the other side various labelled figures in the underworld (Figure 5): at the centre are Hades enthroned and Persephone in a *naiskos* (little shrine), and Dionysos standing just outside the *naiskos* but clasping with his right hand the right hand of Hades. Also outside the *naiskos* are, on the left with Dionysos, two maenads and a satyr called Oinops; underneath is a Paniskos teasing Cerberus; on the right is Hermes, and Aktaion, Pentheus, and Agaue. The handclasp signifies concord: whether, more specifically, it also anticipates arrival or departure or anything else, we cannot say. For the Dionysiac initiate it would surely be reassuring, as indicating that Dionysos, though not himself the ruler, has power in the kingdom of the dead. This close relation is sometimes expressed as kinship: Dionysos, normally the son of Semele, becomes the son of Persephone. Even his enemy (and cousin!) Pentheus seems now untroubled. In a description of the underworld reported by Plutarch (*Moralia* 565–6) there is a very pleasant place like 'Bacchic caves', with 'bacchic revelry and laughter and all kinds of festivity and delight. It was here, said the guide, that Dionysos ascended and later brought up Semele.' The

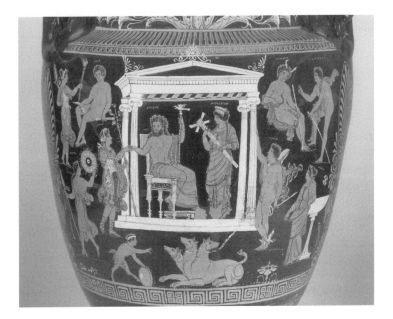

Figure 5 Apulian volute krater painted by the Dareios Painter.

Source: Toledo Museum of Art, Gift of Edward Drummond Libbey, Florence Scott Libbey, and the Egyptian Exploration Society, by exchange, 1994.19

Roman poet Horace (*Odes* 2.19.29–32) imagines the fierce guardian of the underworld, the three-headed dog Cerberus, gently fawning on the departing Dionysos. Dionysos transforms the underworld. Not unnaturally therefore was he brought into relation (sometimes as 'Iakchos') with the chthonian goddesses of the Eleusinian mysteries, Demeter and Korē.

The funerary gold leaf found at Pelinna in Thessaly (late fourth century BC) instructs the dead to 'say to Persephone that Bakchios himself freed you' (see p. 55). Again, Dionysos is not the ruler of the underworld but ensures the well-being of the initiate in the underworld. Why this dual authority? Because the realm and rulers of the underworld are forbidding and remote, and yet we must in this world make the acquaintance of a power that will ensure us happiness in the next. And so this power (Dionysos) must have good relations with the rulers of the underworld, but be less remote. And indeed, as we saw in Chapter 4, Dionysos is more present among humankind, and more intimately related to his adherents, than is any other immortal.

DIONYSIAC INITIATES IN THE UNDERWORLD

Dionysos frees his initiand in the face of death. This is one of various ways in which he liberates (Chapter 3). He liberates psychologically through wine (*Bacchae* 279–83, Plutarch *Moralia* 68d, 716b), but here there may also be anticipation of the next world. On the Pelinna leaf the initiate on the way to the underworld is also told that 'you have wine (as your) *eudaimōn* honour': *eudaimōn* expresses the eternal happiness of the initiate. Wine is consumed in mystery-cult, and various texts refer to the consumption of wine by initiates in the next world (Chapter 5). The satyr in the underworld in our vase in Ohio is, we noted, called 'Oinops' ('Wineface'). It is even imagined – to judge by some Apulian vase-paintings – that in the underworld wine flows miraculously from grapes, without human labour.

Wine in mystic ritual may provide a taste of the next world, as may also the kind of wine-free ecstasy experienced by, for instance, the Theban maenads in *Bacchae* (686–713). We will see (Chapter 8) that Dionysiac mystic initiation may – through the 'right kind of madness' – release initiates from the sufferings both of this world and of the next (Plato *Phaedrus* 244e). We can go further and say that the sufferings of this world and of the next might, in mystic ritual, be one and the same, inasmuch as mystic ritual is a rehearsal for death, so that the sufferings here and now in mystic ritual may have included the terrors of the underworld. A surviving fragment (57) of Aeschylus' lost drama *Edonians* describes a celebration of the Dionysiac thiasos in which the 'semblance of a drum, like subterranean thunder, is carried along, heavily terrifying'. This chthonic (underworld) roar suggests an earthquake. Just before the mystic epiphany of Dionysos to his thiasos in *Bacchae* he calls on 'Mistress Earthquake' to shake the earth. Dionysos then emerges from within the darkness of the house, where the actions of his captor Pentheus are marked by a series of resemblances – too detailed for coincidence – with the description by Plutarch of what mystic initiation has in common with the experience of death, notably light appearing in the darkness (Chapter 5). Harpokration (second century AD) states that those being initiated to Dionysos are crowned with poplar because it belongs to the underworld. The funerary gold leaves from Hipponion and Pelinna record formulae, almost certainly uttered in mystic ritual, that embody instructions to Dionysiac initiates on what to do in the underworld.

Caves are easily imagined as a space between this world and the underworld. And so just as Plutarch compared part of the underworld to 'the Bacchic caves', so conversely caves were in mystic ritual almost certainly sometimes imagined as belonging or leading to the underworld. The earliest suggestion of this is provided by Athenian vase-paintings of the early fourth century BC (discussed by Bérard) that depict an ascent from a subterranean cave in Dionysiac cult (probably mystic initiation). But the association of Dionysos with caves goes back much earlier, for Dionysos was represented in a cave on the chest attributed by Pausanias (5.17.5, 19.6) to the time of the seventh century BC Corinthian tyrant Kypselos. The account of Dionysiac mystery-cult in 186 BC in Livy records that men were transported by a machine into hidden caves and said to have been taken off by the gods (39.13.13). We have seen evidence from Callatis for the use of a cave to simulate the underworld for initiands, and from Latium of 'cave guardians' (p. 67). The late second century AD poet Oppian records that the infant Dionysos' nurses hid him in a cave and 'danced the mystic dance around the child' (*Cynegetica* 4.246).

It was perhaps in an imagined underworld that there occurred the frightening apparitions (*phasmata* and *deimata*) attributed to Dionysiac initiation by Origen (*Against Celsus* 4.10). It was reported that Demosthenes called Aeschines' mother 'Empousa' 'because she appeared out of dark places to those being initiated' (Idomeneus 338 *FrGH* F2): the monster Empousa was one of the terrors encountered by Dionysos in the underworld in Aristophanes' *Frogs*. Any terror inspired by the mystic ritual would eventually yield to the joy of salvation, as described by Plutarch and dramatised in the appearance of Dionysos to his thiasos in *Bacchae*.

It is in the light of this transition to eternal joy that we must see the frequency of satyrs and maenads, who are untouchable by ageing or death, in funerary art throughout antiquity – notably, along with symbols of mystic initiation, in the vase-paintings of fourth-century BC Apulia and from the early second century AD in the sculpted decoration of marble sarcophagi from various parts of the Roman empire. Mystic initiation might mean becoming a member of the mythical thiasos – a nymph, maenad, or satyr (e.g. Plato *Laws* 815) – for all eternity. A Hellenistic epigram from Miletus, mentioned in Chapter 5, honours Alkmeionis, who led the maenads to the mountain and carried the mystic objects (*orgia*) and 'knows her share in good things': this last phrase (*kalōn moiran epistamenē*) refers to the knowledge that she acquired in initiation and has taken with her to the next world.

UNITING THIS WORLD WITH THE NEXT

Dionysos unites the opposites. In mystic ritual he unites this world with the next, liberating his adherents from the sufferings of both, bringing into this world communal well-being that persists into the next. Plato adapted mystic doctrine in the direction of rejecting this world, but Dionysiac mystery-cult as actually practised is other-worldly without being world-denying. Dionysos belongs to both worlds, and moves between the two. A fifth-century BC Olbian bone plate contains the words 'life death life' along with 'Dio<nysos>' (Chapter 5). Plutarch (*Moralia* 565–6, quoted above, p. 79) refers to more than one ascent by Dionysos from the underworld, through a place resembling 'the Bacchic caves'. Similarly, it is up through a cave that we see (almost certainly) Dionysos emerging onto earth in a painting on a *krater* of the early fourth century BC in the British Museum. Pausanias (2.37.5) states that it was through the Alcyonian lake (at Lerna in the Argolid) that Dionysos went down to Hades to bring up his mother Semele, and according to Plutarch (*Moralia* 364f) the Argives called him out of the water with the sound of trumpets, while throwing into the depths a lamb 'for the Gatekeeper'. In one late tradition (*scholium* on *Iliad* 14.319) king Perseus killed Dionysos and threw him into the water at Lerna.

But Dionysos' round trip to the underworld that we know in most detail forms the plot of Aristophanes' *Frogs*. Here the persistence of Dionysiac well-being into the next world takes the extreme form of comedy. Plutarch, we remember, reported 'bacchic revelry and laughter' where Dionysos had passed through the underworld. In the *Frogs* laughter surrounds even the terrors of the underworld (278–311), and moreover – as in the mystic transition that Plutarch compares to the experience of death – these terrors yield to the appearance of a happy chorus of Eleusinian initiates singing a processional hymn to Iakchos, and carrying the 'holy light' of torches (313–459). Dionysos expresses the desire to dance and play with a young girl in the procession (414–5). There is also an invitation by a servant of Persephone, queen of the underworld, to a feast that includes excellent wine as well as girls dancing and playing music (503–18). Dionysos in the underworld is – no doubt like many of his adherents – a cowardly hedonist. Finally, the *communality* of the well-being created by Dionysos (Chapter 3) is evoked in the ending of the play: Aeschylus, declared victor by Dionysos in the poetic contest with Euripides, is escorted back up to the light in order to save Athens.

Another drama set in the underworld was the lost *Sisyphos* by Aeschylus. As a satyr-play, it had a chorus of satyrs who – if they were represented as Dionysiac initiates – corresponded to the chorus of Eleusinian initiates in the underworld in *Frogs*. Another fifth-century play that seems to have been set in the underworld was Aristias' *Keres*. This was probably a satyr-play, in which case the chorus of satyrs were presumably identified with *Keres*, spirits of death. This identification may seem odd: perhaps it was connected with the presence of (men dressed as) satyrs, as well as of the dead, at the Anthesteria, at which was uttered the formula 'Be gone *Keres*, it is no longer Anthesteria'.

THE DEATH OF DIONYSOS

Dionysos is close to humankind through his presence among them and his resemblance to them (dancing, drinking, cowardice), and in fact the resemblance transcends even the most crucial distinction between humankind and deity: Dionysos is *killed*. Although he was generally imagined to be an immortal (and was said to have immortalised his mother Semele), in the sanctuary of Apollo at Delphi there was a tomb inscribed with the words 'Here lies, dead, Dionysos, son of Semele' (Philochorus 328 *FGrH* F7), which implies permanent death. But Plutarch (*Moralia* 365) connects with this tomb both the myth of Dionysos' dismemberment by the Titans and a secret sacrifice 'whenever the Thyiades arouse Liknites'. The Delphic Thyiades are female adherents of Dionysos, and Liknites a title of the god that derives from the *liknon* (mystic basket: Chapter 5). An Orphic Hymn (53) refers to the chthonic (underworld) Dionysos sleeping in the halls of Persephone and being roused 'along with the nymphs' (i.e. his thiasos). The myth of his dismemberment at the hands of the Titans, followed by his restoration to life, is (at least in part) a projection of the experience of the mystic initiand (Chapter 5). The result is that not just his death but also his restoration to life brings him closer to us than are most other deities, and the same can be said even of the *form* of this death and restoration, namely dismemberment (fragmentation) and return to wholeness (see Chapter 8).

The fragmentation of Dionysos is suggested by an Athenian vase-painting, by the 'Eretria Painter', of women bringing offerings to a mask of Dionysos cradled in a *liknon*. The name of the Dionysos aroused by the Thyiads at Delphi (along with a sacrifice at his tomb) derived, we remember, from the *liknon*. In *Bacchae* Agaue in triumphal frenzy carries the head – presumably the mask – of the dismembered Pentheus, her son, over whose reconstituted body she will lament, although here, in pathetic contrast to the myth of Dionysos dismembered, there is no renewed life. The lament of Niobe for her offspring was proverbial. But the lament of Agaue was even more pitiful in that, like other mythical maenads such as the Minyads, she laments a son whom she has herself torn apart. Maenads in a frenzy tear apart their own children, and on realising what they have done become frenzied with grief. Consequently both the savage violence and the lamentation of maenads seem to have been paradigmatic, for in tragedy female murderous savagery and female lamentation are both associated with maenadism, for instance in Euripides' *Hecuba* (686, 1077).

There is considerable evidence (albeit much of it from late antiquity) for lamentation in mystery-cult, sometimes for the deity. The dismemberment of Dionysos was associated with – or perhaps in some way enacted in – his mystery-cult: we know this mainly from late texts, but there is evidence that the myth was known in the archaic and classical periods (Chapters 5 and 8), and in view of our vase-painting of maenads attending the head (mask) of Dionysos in the *liknon*, it is possible that in the fifth century BC maenads in mystery-cult lamented the death of Dionysos. And given the importance of Dionysiac cult – and specifically of mystery-cult performed by the thiasos – in the genesis of Athenian tragedy, it is not unlikely that the centrality of lamentation for an individual in tragedy derives in part from maenadic lamentation. Tragedy comes into being out of – among other things – the confluence of Dionysiac mystery-cult with the kind of death ritual known as hero-cult. This will become clearer in the next chapter.

OVERVIEW

The god who is most associated with exuberant life is also the god who is – apart from Hades himself – most associated with death and the underworld, a paradox first noted by Herakleitos. Dionysos moves between the next world and this one, and is himself killed in a gruesome manner. But none of this implies a belief in the equal power of life and death. In his mystery-cult Dionysos introduces death with its terrors into this world, and is himself killed, so as to give to his initiates experience of the joys that await them in the next world.

7

THEATRE

INTRODUCTION

This chapter is the culmination of the preceding five. Athenian drama originated, and continued for centuries to be performed, in the cult of Dionysos. As we shall see in the course of this chapter, each of the aspects of the cult described in the preceding chapters contributed to the genesis and mature form of one or more of the dramatic genres of tragedy, satyric drama, and comedy.

THE GENESIS OF DRAMA

I begin with communality. Drama came into being in the kind of polis festival of Dionysos that I described in Chapter 3. The oldest Athenian festival of Dionysos was the Anthesteria. But the most important context for the genesis and performance of drama was the sanctuary and theatre of Dionysos Eleuthereus, during his spring festival a month or so later than the Anthesteria, namely the 'Dionysia in the town' (as opposed to the country), generally called 'City Dionysia', which was considerably amplified (if not actually established) at Athens in the second half of the sixth century BC.

It is unsurprising that the unprecedented development of sophisticated drama (tragedy and satyric drama) should have occurred at a new festival rather than at one still celebrated in accordance with ancient tradition. This renewal, which probably occurred during the tyranny of Peisistratus, seems to have been concerned not so much with the traditional seasonal and viticultural elements prominent in the Anthesteria as with the more political aim of displaying the coherence and magnificence of Athens (to itself and to others), and this too may have been a factor in the genesis of drama. Nevertheless, there are some basic similarities, as well as some significant differences, between Anthesteria and City Dionysia.

First the *similarities*. Both festivals are spring festivals in which the whole community participates. Both festivals, it seems, contain processions escorting (an image of) Dionysos from periphery to centre, in the Anthesteria perhaps leading to sexual union with the wife of the 'king' (a magistrate), in the City Dionysia to the theatre. And in both cases this arrival was, naturally enough, associated with myth – in the Anthesteria probably with Dionysos' sexual union with Ariadne and with his liberation from pirates, in the City Dionysia with his original arrival from Eleutherai on the border with Boeotia. These myths account for the rituals that enact them.

Then there are two *differences* that are for our purposes significant. First, there was at the Anthesteria a secret ritual (including sacrifice) performed in the old royal house by a band of women in association with the aforementioned sexual union of Dionysos (Chapters 2 and 5). Similarly, in the meagre surviving evidence for the Lenaia, the other Dionysiac festival at which some drama was performed, there are various indications that mystic ritual was performed by a band of women. And second, at the Anthesteria it seems that large numbers of men and boys participated dressed as satyrs.

Neither of these practices occurred at the City Dionysia. Instead we have the development of drama. I suggest that at the City Dionysia the two missing practices were absorbed into the transformation there of ritual into drama. This is to say that celebrations by men dressed as satyrs, and mystic ritual at the heart of the festival, both contributed to the genesis of drama.

What is the evidence for this? After every set of three tragedies at the City Dionysia there was (in the fifth century BC at least) performed a satyr-play, a burlesque drama with a chorus of boisterous satyrs. There is evidence that tragedy was originally about myths concerning Dionysiac themes, that it soon turned to non-Dionysiac myths, and that satyric drama was established in the festival programme so as to reconcile the audience to the loss of Dionysiac content from tragedy.

Moreover, Aristotle in Chapter 4 of his *Poetics* (by far our best source for the genesis of tragedy) states that tragedy began in improvisation and that it took time to acquire its elevated tone 'because it developed from the satyr-play-like'. He also stated that tragedy developed 'from the leaders of the dithyramb'. This evidence all coheres. The dithyramb was a hymn (originally processional) to Dionysos, that might be performed by satyrs, and indeed at the Athenian Anthesteria it seems that pipe-playing satyrs participated in a festal procession of the kind likely to have been accompanied by the dithyramb. The procession was, moreover, probably followed by the secret ritual in the old royal house.

There is evidence that a crucial step in the transformation of the dithyramb into tragedy was its transformation from a traditional processional hymn into a scripted song sung at a fixed point (the destination of the procession, at an altar, in the city centre rather than at the periphery), along with the increase in solemnity that led to tragedy. In *Bacchae* the song sung by the initiated thiasos which forms the chorus, as they escort Dionysos into the city and take up position around the altar in the orchestra of the theatre, has numerous features of the dithyramb.

The other practice missing from the City Dionysia – because it was absorbed into the development of drama – is mystery-cult, which has left traces in both dithyramb and satyric drama. Mystery-cult contributed to the development of drama something that, though we take it for granted, is in pre-dramatic societies very rare (outside ritual), namely the practice of abandoning your everyday identity to perform in a completely new one. That Dionysiac mystery-cult might take the form of a simple drama is clear from the later inscriptional evidence for it discussed in Chapter 5. In both mystery-cult and Athenian drama the transformation of identity might take the extreme form of transvestism (actors and chorus were all male).

There are two further features of mystery-cult, as described in Chapter 5, that are relevant here. First the mystic initiand might undergo a fictional death (just like the tragic actor) expressed in the actual death of a sacrificial animal ('tragedy' derives its name from song at goat-sacrifice). And second he might be masked and dressed as a satyr. Masks of satyrs and masks of Dionysos predate drama. Of all deities it is Dionysos who is most associated with the mask. For instance, on the François Vase, produced in Athens two generations before the genesis of drama there, he is distinguished by his mask-like face (Chapter 2).

At the Dionysiac festivals the citizens en masse watched the ritual impersonation of myth on the streets, but were excluded from the mystic ritual at the heart of the festival. And so not only was the traditional processional hymn transformed into a scripted stationary hymn under a hillside (so that all could see), but also the irresistibly secret sights of mystic ritual were opened out to the curious gaze of the entire polis. Greek ritual tends to enact its own aetiological myth, and the first tragedies were, I suspect, dramatisations of the aetiological myths enacted in mystery-cult – as was, a century later, the highly traditional *Bacchae*.

But this is not to say that tragedy simply developed out of mystery-cult performed by satyrs. Extant tragedies are sometimes medleys of different kinds of ritual performance, and I suspect that the (unrecoverable) genesis of tragedy involved a fusion of several different kinds of performance: a contribution was probably made by the cult performed at the tombs of heroes, for instance, or even by recitations of Homer. And to this diverse matrix we should also add unprecedented politico-economic factors that cannot be presented here.

Also performed at Athenian festivals of Dionysos was *comedy*, but its genesis was even more unrecoverable than that of tragedy. The Greek word *kōmōidia* (comedy) means 'song sung at a *kōmos*'. *Kōmos* is the word for a kind of revelry associated especially with Dionysos and his festivals. Aristotle derives comedy from 'the leaders of the phallic songs', but has to admit that its early stages are, unlike those of tragedy, unknown. The extent to which the elaborate structure of Aristophanes' plays derives from the structure of a pre-existing ritual is impossible to determine. The kind of song that Aristotle had in mind is exemplified by the phallic song sung in the little rural procession, complete with phallus, celebrated in honour of Dionysos in Aristophanes' *Acharnians* (241–79). The Dionysiac rituals performed at Athens were of various kinds, and the differences – and complementarity – between them contributed to the differences – and complementarity – between the dramatic genres to the genesis of which they contributed.

DRAMA ABOUT DIONYSOS

The first dramatist of whom complete plays have survived is Aeschylus (525–456 BC). None of these extant plays are about Dionysos, but of the sixty or so titles of tragedies ascribed to Aeschylus two may well have been about Dionysos (*Athamas* and *Toxotides*) and seven certainly were: *Semele, Xantriai, Pentheus, Bacchae, Edonians, Bassarids, Neaniskoi*. It is possible that *Semele, Xantriai*, and *Pentheus* formed a connected trilogy. Such a trilogy would have dramatised the events leading up to, and including, the death of Pentheus as dramatised in Euripides' *Bacchae*. Almost nothing survives from these plays, but we know that they contained the appearance of Hera (as enemy of Semele and Dionysos), and of *Lyssa* (Frenzy) inspiring the maenads. And it seems that whoever touched the belly of Semele when she was pregnant with Dionysos was thereby possessed by the god. The birth of Dionysos must have been a striking event, even if only narrated. Accompanied by the thunder and lightning that destroyed his mother Semele, it was associated with (and probably somehow experienced in) mystic initiation, and was accordingly both a common theme of the dithyramb and prominent in Euripides' *Bacchae* (3, 6–12, 42, 88–103, 243–5, 286–97, 512–29, 597–9, 623–4). The most substantial fragment of the *Edonians* refers (probably in a dithyrambic entry-song) to the terrifying sound of drums as of thunder under the earth.

Bacchae attributed to Aeschylus may have been an alternative name for his *Pentheus*. The *Edonians* dramatised the vain resistance of the Thracian king Lykourgos to the newly arrived Dionysos and probably also the victory of Dionysos and punishment of Lykourgos. Its surviving fragments suggest that the play resembled Euripides' *Bacchae* not just in plot but also in details. It was followed by *Bassarids* and *Neaniskoi* in a connected trilogy. The Bassarids were Thracian maenads, sent by Dionysos to dismember Orpheus. This was because Orpheus, as a result of visiting the underworld (to find his wife), abandoned his loyalty to Dionysos and instead regarded the sun as the greatest of the gods, calling it Apollo. It seems that Orpheus experienced a bright light in the darkness of the underworld, and that this was – like the light in darkness experienced by Pentheus in *Bacchae* (Chapter 5) – a mythical projection of a similar experience in mystic initiation. For mystic initiation, being a pre-enactment of death, frequently involved the experience of a bright light (identified with a saving person, the 'Being of Light') in the darkness of death, and in this and other respects resembles the cross-cultural Near-Death Experience (Chapter 5). The theme of the third drama in the trilogy, the *Neaniskoi*, is unknown. It has been suggested that it restored the balance by the foundation of cult for Orpheus and Apollo.

Of plays about Dionysos by Sophokles and Euripides not much is known, apart from Euripides' *Bacchae*. Tragedies were written about Dionysos by minor tragedians. Polyphrasmon wrote a trilogy about Dionysos and Lykourgos (467 BC). Titles that appear more than once are *Bacchae* and *Semele*, and there was a tragedy (by Spintharos) entitled *Semele Thunderbolted* (*Semele Keraunoumenē*).

Dionysos also made some appearances in the other two dramatic genres over which he presided as god of the festival, satyric drama and comedy. Although the chorus of satyric drama consisted always of his thiasos of satyrs, the god himself seems to have been generally absent, especially as the satyrs were often the captives of some uncongenial master – as for example in the only satyr-play that survives complete, Euripides' *Cyclops*, in which they are the slaves of the giant Polyphemos in Sicily. In the prologue the arrival of the chorus of satyrs reminds Silenos of their earlier sexy dancing to the sound of the deep-toned lyre when once as a band of revellers they escorted Dionysos to the house of his paramour Althaia. This happy event had probably been dramatised in a satyr-play now lost. An intriguing example of a lost satyr-play containing Dionysos himself is Sophokles' *Dionysiskos* ('Little Dionysos'), in which the satyrs express their delight at the invention of wine by the infant Dionysos.

Of surviving comedies, Dionysos plays a central part – albeit an unheroic one – in Aristophanes' *Frogs* (405 BC). As for lost comedies, their surviving titles show that Dionysos appeared frequently in Old Comedy, and occasionally we get more than a glimpse of his presence.

In Eupolis' *Taxiarchoi* (Officers) he went to learn the arts of war from the general Phormion. One fragment of the comic poet Hermippus (63) provides a list of the numerous things that Dionysos brings to Athens in his ship from around the eastern Mediterranean, and another (77) has him describing and judging various wines. In Cratinus' *Dionysalexandros* the satyrs accompanied Dionysos in an amorous adventure, this time with Helen. And so we have now seen the heterosexual union of Dionysos being enacted not only in the Anthesteria and (probably) in satyric drama, but also in Old Comedy. And it also occurred in the simple drama, or 'tableau', described by Xenophon (*Symposium* 9.2–7) as performed at a symposium set in 421 BC: Ariadne, dressed as a bride, is approached by Dionysos to the 'Bacchic rhythm' of the pipe, and after they embrace and she affirms her love for him, they retire to bed, to the excitement of the onlookers.

This erotic show at a drinking party suggests that it was in particular Dionysos who inspired the kind of abandon that favoured the occurrence of simple drama in contexts other than the theatre. The celebrations of Dionysiac associations were one such context (Chapter 5). Diodorus (4.3) describes the practice in many Greek cities of women 'generally hymning the *presence* of Dionysos, *imitating* the maenads who were the companions of the god' (my emphases). A late text (scholiast on Aristides 22, 20) tells us that 'in the processions one man took the appearance of Dionysos, another of Satyr, another of Bakchos'. And consider the revelry (in 48 AD) of the emperor Claudius' wife Messalina (Tacitus *Annals* 11.31). There was an imitation (*simulacrum*) of the vintage, with wine-presses and flowing vats of wine. Maenads dressed in skins were leaping as if sacrificing or in a frenzy. Messalina herself with unloosed hair was shaking a thrysos next to her ivy-crowned lover Silius, and around them was the harsh sound of a chorus. Vettius Valens climbed a tall tree, from which he saw a storm coming from Ostia. Just as Silius seems to be Dionysos (and Messalina Ariadne?), so Vettius Valens was perhaps Pentheus, who in *Bacchae* is set on top of a tall tree, ostensibly to enable him to see the (hostile) maenads.

IS ATHENIAN DRAMA DIONYSIAC?

Athenian drama of the classical period derived in part from Dionysiac ritual, and was Dionysiac in its spatial and temporal context. It was performed in a sanctuary of Dionysos along with rituals for Dionysos (notably a procession leading animals to be sacrificed in the sanctuary) during a festival of Dionysos. Dionysos is often regarded as a source of poetic inspiration, and associated with the Muses. In Aristophanes' *Frogs* Dionysos is throughout the plot closely associated with tragedy, and Aeschylus is called 'the Bacchic lord' (1259). Aeschylus' plays are 'full of Dionysos' (Plutarch *Moralia* 715). Dionysos, in legend, told Aeschylus to write tragedy, and protected the dead Sophokles (Pausanias 1.21.1–2).

However, in most Athenian drama of which we know the plot Dionysos does not appear. Is there anything Dionysiac about their content? Satyric drama always has Dionysos' companions as its chorus, and they exhibit the boisterous adherence to (or nostalgia for) the pleasures – of wine, dance, music, and sex – that are dear also to their absent master. In Euripides' *Cyclops* the absence of Dionysos is (as probably in other satyr-plays) felt as a loss, and once liberated from Polyphemos they look forward – in the last line of the drama – to rejoining permanently the service of Dionysos. As for comedy, various of its characteristics – phallic costume, crude sensual pleasures, light-heartedness, vitriolic language, laughter, unrestrainedness, obscenity, revelry – are characteristic also of a kind of celebration associated with Dionysos.

Tragedy, on the other hand, is far removed from the boisterousness and low pleasures of the other two dramatic genres. True, it originated in, and was performed at, a festival of Dionysos, and certain of its features may derive from the Dionysiac ritual that contributed to its genesis. These features are masks, frequent evocation of ritual, the social marginality (as of maenads) of the people represented by the chorus, the centrality (nevertheless) of the chorus to the performance, the tendency of the chorus to associate its own dancing with Dionysos, perhaps even the centrality of a suffering individual. But they are not enough to allow us to characterise as 'Dionysiac' a genre in which Dionysos himself appears only occasionally.

Is there anything else Dionysiac about the content of tragedy? It may seem obvious that the answer is no. But the question raises a broad issue. Greek deities are human constructions. We should always ask what were the human desires or needs that gave rise to this particular deity, or to this particular characteristic or action of a deity. An answer may sometimes be impossible, or at least extremely complex – for instance if the needs and desires forming the deity do not cohere. But we should always ask the question.

What were the human needs or desires that formed Dionysos? We have identified the need to express respect and gratitude for the mysterious power of wine, and the need of the community to express its unity. These two sources for the construction of Dionysos may cohere, inasmuch as wine dissolves the psychological barriers between individuals, thereby fostering community. But this power to dissolve the boundaries of the individual is required also for the collective frenzy of the Dionysiac thiasos, as well as for the mystic initiation of the individual into the thiasos. Fundamental to Dionysiac mystic initiation is radical transformation of identity. This transformation may involve the temporary dissolution of the boundaries between male and female, between human and animal, and – above all – between life and death. And the epiphany of the deity may serve both as a focus for the unity of thiasos or of community and as the embodiment of salvation for the terrified initiand.

The preceding paragraph has indicated the coherence of the preceding five chapters. But there is another striking and characteristic action of Dionysos in myth. When people resist the introduction of his cult, he inspires them into a frenzy in which they kill their own kin (e.g. the daughters of Minyas, Lykourgos), and the cult is established. This sequence was dramatised in Euripides' *Bacchae*, probably also in Aeschylus' *Edonians*. The self-destruction (albeit inspired by Dionysos) of the autocratic family leads to cult for the whole community. The pattern frequently occurs, albeit without the presence of Dionysos, in tragedy (although both elements of it are alien to Homer). To take just two examples: in Euripides' *Hippolytus* Theseus is responsible for the death of his son Hippolytus, whose cult in Trozen is predicted by Artemis at the end of the play. And in his *Herakles*, Herakles in a frenzy kills his own children, and on regaining sanity is finally led away to Athens where he will receive hero-cult celebrated by the whole polis (1332–3). This pattern of action originated, I suggest, in the Dionysiac themes – in which it is most at home – of the earliest tragedies: Dionysos, god of frenzy and community, inspired kin-killing and founded communal cult. The pattern was then transmitted to subsequent tragedies in which Dionysos himself does not appear.

This hypothesis is supported by another characteristic of tragedy. Even in plays in which Dionysos does not appear, he may be evoked for his association with our pattern. For instance in Euripides' *Herakles*, Herakles is put into a frenzy by Hera and kills his own children, and the frenzy is several times described in Dionysiac terms. Indeed the use of Dionysiac terms for kin-killing frenzy is not infrequent in tragedy, as when – to give another example – Klytaimestra is in Aeschylus' *Agamemnon* called (by an almost certain emendation) 'a raving maenad of Hades, breathing truceless war against her kin; how she raised a shriek of triumph, all-daring, as if at the turn of battle' (compare the warrior maenads of *Bacchae*). Although it was not Dionysos who made Klytaimestra kill her husband, we feel that 'maenad' here may be more than a mere metaphor.

Moreover, that the maenadic Klytaimestra should be described as a male (warrior) points to another feature of tragedy that may be inherited from its Dionysiac origin. This is the tendency in tragedy for the boundaries between opposite identities to be dissolved, so that a person may be both male and female, human and animal, even living and dead. These are the three boundaries dissolved (polarities confused) in Dionysiac initiation, along with the stubborn boundary separating the individual psyche from the group. And all four dissolutions are prominent in the mythical projection of Dionysiac initiation dramatised in *Bacchae*. But they also tend to occur in tragedy even without any mention of Dionysos, for instance in the so-called 'deception speech' in Sophokles' *Ajax*.

I conclude that tragedy can be called Dionysiac (even where Dionysos is not mentioned) in the limited sense that it often represents such processes as tend to be imagined as caused by Dionysos: reversal of identity, the frenzied killing of kin (the self-destruction of the household), the (fictional) death of an individual surrounded by a group (thiasos, chorus), leading to cult for the whole community. The human need to represent these processes is expressed in the idea that they are inspired or demanded by Dionysos. But it is also expressed in tragedies, whether or not Dionysos himself appears in them and whether or not we choose to call them Dionysiac.

What is the source of this human need? There is the need for transformation of identity in the face of death, expressed in mystic initiation, and the need for a community to feel itself united. I suggest that tragedy also develops the *political* significance latent in Dionysiac myth. Dionysos had long been associated with the dissolution of boundaries inherent in the communality of the thiasos or of the whole community, which required the departure of the women from their households. And this departure was easily – especially in the extremist logic of myth – imagined as rejection of the enclosed household for the open space of communal celebration. Loyalty to thiasos or polis seems to threaten loyalty to household. Further, the transformation of identity required for joining the initiated community (thiasos) might require the individual to be subjected, in the process of initiation, to a fictional death. These tensions, between household and community and between individual suffering and the well-being of the community, come to express something new – a political transition from tyrannical rule to the communal well-being of polis cult. This scheme is clearest in *Bacchae*, with the 'tyrant' Pentheus vainly resisting the new cult and so killed by his maenadic mother. But it is also to be found in tragedies that are not about Dionysos himself.

The Athenian tyranny was overthrown in 510 BC, a crucial time in the genesis of tragedy at the festival of Dionysos Eleuthereus, at which every year was re-enacted the epiphanic arrival of an outsider (Dionysos) – a ritual conducive to political unity (Chapter 4). The festival also contained the proclamation – probably throughout most of the fifth century – of a reward for killing any of the tyrants (one of many signs of the Athenian democracy's fear of tyranny). In the only surviving tragedy in which Dionysos appears, he is escorted in from outside, inspires the tyrannical family to destroy itself, and founds his cult, all by means of that unique epiphanic intimacy with human beings (Chapter 4) and power of impersonation (himself as priest, Pentheus as maenad) that made his cult conducive to the genesis of drama.

This is not to say that the audience of tragedy simply rejoiced over the demise of the powerful individual and the self-destruction of the tyrannical household. The Dionysiac dissolution of the psychic boundary between stubborn individual and group might draw in not just the chorus but also the entire theatre, and it is in this respect perhaps that theatre may be most profoundly Dionysiac. In tragedy such dissolution might produce collective lamentation for the suffering individual, but this was perfectly consistent with a (conscious or unconscious) sense of satisfaction at the transition from the dangerous excess of the tragic autocrat to the foundation of civic cult, which in some cases perpetuated the communal lamentation for the tragic individual (hero-cult). Communal lamentation enhances communal solidarity, and anyway tears – the Greeks were well aware – are pleasurable.

DIONYSOS AND DRAMA AFTER THE FIFTH CENTURY BC

Although not much Greek drama survives from after the fifth century BC, we do know that throughout antiquity it retained its original association with Dionysos. Two kinds of evidence for this association are especially interesting: (i) vase-painting from southern Italy, notably Apulia, and (ii) the inscriptional evidence for the guilds of performers called Artists of Dionysos.

(i) Numerous Apulian painted vases of the fourth century BC have been discovered in tombs (Chapter 6). As might be expected of painting placed in tombs, much of it seems to embody hope for the afterlife. Many of these paintings are of myths, or at least of individuals from myth. Some of these individuals seem to have eschatological significance, such as Herakles, Protesilaos, or Orpheus, each of whom returned from the underworld. And in a few pictures it seems that the dead person is identified with a mythological figure. Even where there is no obvious eschatological significance, depictions of deities and heroes sometimes seem to have the aim of absorbing the dead into the heroic-divine world. On the Dionysiac funerary gold leaves (Chapter 5) from roughly the same time and place (southern Italy) there occur the mystic formulae 'you became a god instead of a man' and 'and then afterwards you will rule [among the other] heroes'. In one Apulian vase-painting (by the Baltimore painter, in a private collection in Paris) it seems that the tent of Achilles is assimilated to the palace of Hades.

Experiencing myth was important in the ancient enactment of ritual, not least of death ritual. For instance, in the *Iliad* Achilles recounts the myth of Niobe mourning her twelve children as a paradigm for the mourning which he and Priam are engaged in (even Niobe, despite her extreme grief, did eventually eat), and this myth was also a theme of Apulian vase-painting. This use of myth was sufficiently fundamental to survive into Christianity – for instance in the Greek belief that the funeral feast originated in the instructions given from the Cross by Christ to his mother to prepare the funeral feast despite her grief. As might be expected, it seems that words of consolation were – from at least as early as the fourth century BC – sometimes delivered at private funerals, although no such speeches have survived. A late rhetorical treatise recommends the consoling power of myth at funerals, for example of the myth of Achilles at the funeral of a young man. And Lucian provides evidence for funerary songs about 'ancient disasters' (*On Grief* 20).

Some of the paintings of myth – perhaps more of them than may at first appear – are inspired by dramatic performances. It has been cogently argued that several scenes from tragedy have been chosen – or even reshaped – by the painter so as to imply the hope of life after death. An example is provided by paintings of Andromeda tied up but about to be rescued from imminent death and married, which was the theme of famous tragedies by Sophokles and Euripides. Even the numerous tragic myths that end badly may serve to soften human suffering by providing it with even greater suffering (for contrast) or with noble associations. Many (if not all) of the surviving Apulian vase-paintings of Niobe are influenced by Aeschylus' tragic *Niobe*. The fourth-century BC Athenian Timokles wrote a comedy entitled *Women at the Dionysia*, from which a passage survives describing the usefulness of tragedy: various forms of human misery can be relieved by contemplating figures in tragedy who are in an even worse state: 'Someone's child has died, Niobe is a comfort. Someone is lame, he sees Philoktetes', and so on (fragment 6 *PCG*).

What made the dead take myths from *tragedy* with them into the underworld was, I suspect, not just their reassuring quality but its powerful combination with the lasting impression made by their theatrical performance. It is especially in tragedy that myth comes to life. The vases often have paintings of the underworld that have the same compositional structure as the paintings inspired by dramatic performances. These scenes of the underworld also sometimes contain tragic costumes, and symbols associated with Dionysiac mystery-cult.

Another especially common theme of Apulian funerary vases is Dionysos, his retinue, and his symbols. We have already seen evidence for the popularity of Dionysiac mystery-cult, with its hope for well-being in the underworld, in southern Italy (Chapters 5 and 6). Inasmuch as Dionysos is also the god of tragedy, here is another potential factor in the salvational associations of scenes from tragedy. In order to illustrate the salvational co-existence of the theatrical and the Dionysiac I will now describe the themes painted on an Apulian volute krater of about 330 BC (illustrated in Oliver Taplin, *Comic Angels*, Plate 5), chosen somewhat arbitrarily from many similar vase-paintings.

The main scene on one side shows several figures, divine and human, taken from the story of the escape of Phrixos and Helle from the threat of being sacrificed as the result of the hostility of their stepmother Ino. The moment chosen is when it seems that Phrixos and Helle are beginning to suspect that it is they themselves – and not the ram at the altar – who are threatened by the knife held by their father Athamas. Soon the golden-fleeced ram will bear them away through the sky. This was a popular theme of Athenian tragedy in the fifth and fourth centuries BC.

The main scene on the other side shows a funerary *naiskos* – a small shrine-like structure on a plinth, with an Ionian column on either side, crowned by a pediment. Inside the *naiskos* is a young man standing naked, and outside it are six figures, three on either side, each carrying one or more ritual objects. Above this scene, painted on the neck of the vase, is a flowery meadow in which a naked seated young man holds in one hand a *thyrsos* and in the other a vessel into which liquid – presumably wine – is pouring automatically from two bunches of grapes. On one side of him is a winged female figure and on the other a satyr, each carrying ritual objects. Whereas the main scene shows the deceased young man in his funerary *naiskos*, surrounded by mortals calmly bringing him offerings, the scene above it shows him surrounded by immortals in a Dionysiac paradise – if indeed the seated young man there is the deceased and not Dionysos himself (or he could conceivably be the former imagined as the latter). The automatic flow of wine implies a world without labour. And as we saw in Chapter 6, the consumption of wine was an important feature of the next world for the initiated. A passage by the comic poet Pherecrates (fragment 113) implies that the supply of wine in Hades is unlimited.

This vase may have been used in the funeral ceremony (for libations or at a feast), was buried with the dead, and depicts the deceased both within his funerary monument and (it seems) in the Dionysiac afterlife. And so it is difficult to believe that the other main theme, Phrixos and Helle and their imminent miraculous escape over the sea from violent death, was arbitrarily chosen. The combination of tragic myth with the Dionysiac is common in Apulian vase-paintings but not confined to them. For instance, it has been noted that the kalyx-kraters found on the island of Lipari (off the north coast of Sicily) 'throughout intertwine iconographical motifs from the theatre with those of specific Dionysiac cult rituals, including in several instances the presence of the god himself' (Eva Keuls).

(ii) After having developed in Attica, drama spread throughout much of the Greek-speaking world, which was hugely expanded by the conquests of Alexander the Great (356–323 BC). As a result, the performers of drama tended to become professionals who may be hired by various cities. From the early third century BC, and for six centuries thereafter, we find evidence (mostly inscriptional) of guilds of performers, called *Technitai* ('Artists' or 'Artisans') of Dionysos, organising the affairs and representing the interests of the performers. We learn much about such matters as the organisation, payment, status, and mobility of the performers. But our interest here is in the fact that the deity most honoured by the associations is Dionysos. As well as being concerned with the interests of their members, these are religious associations, proud of their 'piety'.

There is moreover some evidence that – like other Dionysiac associations – the *Technitai* performed mystery-cult. We have seen Dionysiac associations, formed by initiation, impersonating Dionysos' mythical associates as well as performing dramas, and at Smyrna an association of '*technitai* (i.e. actors) and *mustai* (mystic initiates) around Dionysos Breiseus' (Chapter 5). An inscribed decree of 78–7 BC refers to the Athenian *Technitai* of Dionysos having established an altar and sanctuary at Eleusis where they performed libations and paeans, and offered sacrifice and libations to Demeter and Korē on the days of the mysteries. And an inscribed decree from Ancyra, of the ecumenical *Technitai* of Dionysos under the emperor Hadrian, refers to a 'mystic contest (*mustikos agōn*)' and to 'every part of the mystery (*mustērion*)' (*IGR* 3.209). In a passage generally taken to refer to the City Dionysia Alkiphron (second or third century AD) imagines the playwright Menander (circa 342–293 BC) as desiring 'to hymn Dionysos every year at his hearth-altar (*eschara*), to perform the rites of mystery-cult (*mustēriōtidas teletas*), to bring out a new drama at the yearly stage-performances (*thumelais*)' (4.18.16).

Both kinds of evidence just discussed, Apulian funerary vase-painting and inscriptions about the *Technitai* of Dionysos, indicate a close relationship between drama and mystery-cult. There are three important respects in which these two kinds of performance resemble each other. First, at the culmination of mystic ritual there was, as Plato and others make clear, something *seen*, a spectacle. Second, I have argued that – in celebrations that existed before drama – it was above all in mystic ritual that *change of identity* was to be found, and that mystic ritual was an important factor in the genesis of drama. Third, much of what is imitated in tragedy and satyr play (and even in Old Comedy) is *above the human level*. Drama, like mystery-cult, tends to reveal important truths about deities.

As well as resembling each other, mystery-cult and drama interpenetrate. Mystery-cult frequently involved ritual impersonation (of deities, satyrs, etc.), and what was enacted was no doubt generally mythical, for instance the search for Persephone in the Eleusinian mysteries. Clement of Alexandria, who was born in the middle of the second century AD, had probably been initiated into the Dionysiac mysteries before his conversion to Christianity. He writes in his *Protrepticus* (II) that 'as for your so-called gods who have mystic initiations, I will wheel them out (*ekkuklēsō*), as if on the stage of life for the spectators of truth'. This alludes to a theatrical device (the *ekkuklēma*), and implies, as do other Church fathers, the theatricality of mystery-cult. Demeter and Korē, he goes on to say, 'have become a mystic drama'.

The connection of Dionysos with the theatre continues throughout antiquity, so that for example as late as the sixth century AD Choricius of Gaza can entitle his defence of mimes 'On behalf of Those who Represent Life in the Theatre of Dionysos'. But this does not mean that Dionysos was taken seriously – or even thought of at all – by theatre-goers. In 363 AD the emperor Julian ('the apostate') complains of the licentiousness of theatres: he would like, he says, to return them, purified, to Dionysos, but realises that this is impossible (*Letter* 89). However, the frequency and vehemence of Christian denunciations of theatre, often for its immorality but sometimes for its idolatry, suggest that it was – although not necessarily imagined as religious experience – nevertheless sensed as rivalling the performance of Christian liturgy. For it might, like the liturgy, arouse mass emotion in enacting the relationship between man and deity, while outdoing the liturgy in sensual sophistication and social embeddedness. The theatre, complains the Christian Tertullian (c. 160–c. 240 AD), belongs to Venus and Liber, and elsewhere he calls it *ecclesia diaboli* (the church of the devil). For Augustine (354–430 AD), the gods by demanding public stagings of their own misdeeds admit themselves to be unclean spirits (*City of God* 2.26).

Part of the sensual sophistication of the theatre was in its dancing. In the second century AD the pagan Lucian wrote an essay defending dancing (in pantomime, often on themes from tragedy), in which he refers to the enormous popularity of public dances (in Ionia and Pontus) in which 'Titans, Korybantes, Satyrs, and *Boukoloi*' (cowherds: cf. above, 67–8) were proudly impersonated by leading citizens, and describes dance (presumably with some credibility) as 'a divine practice and a mystic one and taken seriously by so many gods and performed in their honour' (*On the Dance* 79, 23). We have seen (Chapter 5) that the dancing in Dionysiac mystery-cult prefigured the joy of the next world. In the end, the church succeeded not only in abolishing mystery-cult but also in separating dance (as well as theatre) from religion, thereby making it difficult for us to appreciate the naturalness of their ancient unity.

OVERVIEW

Drama developed within the cult of Dionysos, and Dionysiac ritual was an important factor in its genesis.

Dionysos is not infrequent as a character in Attic drama. But even some of those tragedies in which he does not appear exhibit a form analogous to, and influenced by, the dramatisation of Dionysiac myth.

Moreover, drama retains its association with Dionysos until after the rise of Christianity. Two of the most abundant manifestations of this association, Apulian vase-painting and inscriptions of the Artists of Dionysos, both also show an association between drama and mystery-cult.

8

PSYCHOLOGY AND PHILOSOPHY

INTRODUCTION

It was claimed in the preceding chapter that Dionysiac mystery-cult was an important factor in the genesis of tragedy. In this chapter a connection will be made between Dionysiac mystery-cult and another Greek invention, philosophy. This connection has two strands, one deriving from the status of mystery-cult as a source of wisdom, the other from the importance of the soul in mystery-cult. In order to understand this latter connection, as well as to develop further the affinity of Donysiac mystery-cult to tragedy, we must first describe the phenomenon of psychological possession.

PSYCHOLOGICAL POSSESSION

The abnormal mental states that occurred in Dionysiac cult are comparable to those that still occur today, in various cultures, in possession cults such as the *candomblé* in Brazil or the Hausa *bori*. Typical manifestations of possession trance that occurred also in Dionysiac cult are trembling, foaming at the mouth, distorted eyes, insensitivity to pain, falling to the ground, imagined death, amnesia, bodily movements such as the arched back with head flung back, and the vital role of music and dance. Moreover, inasmuch as possession trance involves a change of identity, it often takes the form of initiation, which brings the initiate into a relation with a spirit or god that can subsequently be renewed and negotiated and that is a *cure*. There are enough similarities between possession cult in general and the fragmentary evidence for Dionysiac cult to mean that the latter can be cautiously illuminated by the former. This applies in particular to some remarks by Plato.

Plato notes that mothers calm their babies not by stillness but by rocking and a kind of singing, and compares this, as a cure, to the effect of dance and song on those who are 'out of their mind' in a Dionysiac frenzy. In both cases the state to be remedied is a kind of fear, which is by external motion transformed into peace (*galēnē*) and calm (*hēsuchia*) in the soul (*Laws* 790e).

Elsewhere Plato claims that 'our greatest blessings come through madness, provided that it is given as a divine gift' (*Phaedrus* 244a9). When certain families inherit disease and suffering as punishment for ancient transgression, one kind of divine madness 'by encountering initiations (*teletai*) and purifications makes the mad person sound for the present and the time to come, and finds release from present sufferings for the person possessed and frenzied in the right way' (244e). Madness may arise from human diseases or alternatively from 'divine release from customary habits' (265), and so being 'possessed and frenzied in the right way' refers to divine rather than human madness: it is what Plato calls initiatory (*telestikē*) madness, which he ascribes to Dionysos (265).

Comparison to the possession cults of other cultures (in particular to the 'pre-possession crisis') helps us to see that for Plato the disease caused by ancient transgression is (though by implication divinely caused) 'human' in the sense that it is *unritualised* madness, corresponding to the natural agitation of babies, that finds release through the ritual of initiation into the musically controlled movement of Dionysiac trance. But it is in fact natural and common to suppose that the initial, painful crisis of madness is also (unritualised) possession by the spirit or god, as it is sometimes in Dionysiac myth – for instance when the women of Argos are frenzied by Dionysos (and then cured by the Dionysiac priest Melampous). This is so also in other ancient possession cults, such as that of the Korybantes, who both impose and cure madness.

Pindar (fragment 131) refers to *lusiponoi teletai* (mystic initiations that release from suffering). The Roman polymath Varro described the rituals of Liber Pater (Dionysos) as 'pertaining to the purgation of the soul'. And Byzantine scholarship explains the phrase *lusioi teletai* ('mystic initiations that liberate') as 'those of Dionysos'. The various ways in which Dionysos *liberates* (Chapter 3), for instance from imprisonment, include liberation through mystic initiation. And what Dionysos liberates his initiates from includes presumably the madness that Plato describes as arising from ancient transgression and from human diseases.

All this illuminates, I suggest, Teiresias' statement early in *Bacchae* (326) to Pentheus that 'you are mad in the most painful way'. Pentheus persists in his accustomed habits. He is suffering from the painful human kind of madness, and stubbornly resists the new kind offered to him by Dionysos. His subsequent agitation – we have seen – resembles in detail the experience of mystic initiation described in Plutarch, but in horrific contrast to that experience he stubbornly attacks the light that brings salvation (Chapter 5). That is to say, he persists in his state of painful human madness, with the result that the subsequent insertion into him of 'light frenzy' by Dionysos (850–1) will lead only to his destruction. Similarly the frenzy of Agaue, though imposed by Dionysos, also ends in suffering, for she too had transgressed by resisting him (26–33), as had other mythical figures such as Lykourgos and the daughters of Minyas and of Proitos.

As Pentheus first appears on stage, he is described (214) as 'in a flutter' (*eptoëtai*), and the same word is used later in the play (1268) of the 'fluttering' that is 'with the soul (*psūchē*)' of Agaue as she is brought out of the frenzy in which she tore apart her own son. It is used also in a later text of the state of mind of the 'more ignorant' people that is caused by their lives and is purified in Dionysiac initiation by means of songs, dances, and playfulness (Aristides Quintilianus *De Musica* 3.25). Similar words, also meaning 'flutter', are used of the *psūchē* of the initiand in a scene of mock-mystic initiation in Aristophanes (*Clouds* 319), and of the *psūchē* that at death flutters painfully around the body because unwilling to leave it (Plato *Phaedo* 108b1). Some Greek vase-paintings depict the soul leaving the body as a bird. The souls (*psūchai*) of the dead on their way to Hades are compared in

Homer (*Odyssey* 24.1–9) to flitting bats, and in Sophokles to birds (*OT* 174). The idea of the soul fluttering around the body at death, and therefore also in mystic initiation (a rehearsal for death), may be a vestige of the idea of the soul-bird. If so, it has taken on a *subjective* content, for fluttering may be internally felt.

Combining our passages of Plato and *Bacchae*, we may infer that the painful human suffering or disease from which Dionysos liberated or purified his initiands may sometimes have been expressed in a mental fluttering or agitation, and that Dionysiac initiation included both a disruptive reversal of identity (and so of accustomed habits) and a concomitant intensification of the agitation to the point at which it could – by means of music and dance – finally be transformed into divine calm, the *hēsuchia* of Dionysos himself (*Bacchae* 622, 647). And so Dionysiac liberation, producing calm, may have been imagined as not only from painful mental agitation but also from its intensification in the ritual itself. In contrast to the fluttering agitation of Pentheus, the maenads on the mountainside are gentle and calm, a 'wonder to see of good order' (693), like a rising flock of (non-fluttering) birds (748) – it is only when faced with male hostility that they become catastrophically aggressive. In a vase-painting (*ARV²* 16.14) a maenad pulling Pentheus apart is labelled *galēnē*, the word used by Plato (see above, p. 106) of Dionysiac calm.

'Possession' of someone by a spirit or god may take various forms: control, invasion, intimate co-existence, replacement, identification. The verb for 'possessed' at Plato *Phaedo* 244e (quoted above) is *katechein*, 'hold down, occupy', which is used also of what Dionysos does to Agaue in *Bacchae* (1124). Dionysos may also 'take hold of' (*lambanei*) people (Herodotus 4.79), and inspire prophecy by 'entering the body abundantly' (*Bacchae* 300). Maenads may have 'god in them' (*entheoi*: Sophokles *Antigone* 963). But although there survive some indications of the identification of the mystic initiate with Dionysos (Chapter 5), we do not hear of strong forms of identification such as the god (or spirit) speaking in the voice of the possessed. Dionysos is unusually close to people, but after all belongs also to remote Olympos and is a god of the polis.

Though a god of the polis, Dionysos was also imagined to be of foreign (Phrygian) origin, and Dionysiac frenzy was associated especially with the Phrygian musical mode and the Phrygian pipe (*aulos*). A study of the relations between music and possession (by G. Rouget) compares this Phrygian origin with the Gun tribespeople (of Benin) possessed by Yoruba divinities and singing Yoruba songs, or in South Africa the Thonga possessed by Zulu or Ndau spirits and singing Zulu or Ndau songs. Another comparative study (by I. M. Lewis) regards alien spirits as symptomatic of 'marginal' possession cults that have a special appeal to the downtrodden and especially to women. This is exemplified, he believes, in the appeal of possession by the alien Dionysos to women.

But this theory must, if it is to apply to Dionysos, be qualified. We can say that – notably in *Bacchae* – women, isolated in the home and excluded from the structures of power, are impelled by a supposedly foreign deity to form, outside the city, a community that is (still) unstructured and yet cohesive. This is also an aetiological myth of a central cult of the polis. If Dionysos was ever antithetical to the male-dominated polis, that was good reason for him, like the Furies in Aeschylus' *Eumenides*, to be given a central place in polis cult. The association of Dionysia with Phrygia may derive from a combination of three factors: actual influence from Phrygian cult, the ritual of epiphanic arrival from elsewhere (Chapter 4), and the marginality of Dionysos' frenzied adherents.

The phenomenon of possession in mystic initiation seems to have contributed to two momentous achievements that we attribute to the Greeks, tragedy and philosophy.

On tragedy I will be brief. In Chapter 7 I argued that the *change of identity* of the Dionysiac mystic initiand was a factor in the development of tragedy out of Dionysiac mystic initiation. Now we may add that the comparative evidence and the evidence provided by Plato both suggest that the change of identity effected in Dionysiac initiation might have taken the form of possession trance. Moreover, in *Bacchae* Pentheus is put into a 'light frenzy' and *dressed up* as a female in a scene that embodies various details of mystic initiation. Comparative evidence also demonstrates the importance of recognition by the group ('theatralization') of the individual's change of identity in possession trance (G. Rouget), as well as the tendency, in living traditions of masked drama (Japanese and Balinese) and even occasionally in the West, for the new identity embodied in the (physically restrictive) mask to produce an altered state of consciousness (even trance) in the actor (M. J. Coldiron). That these phenomena may, I suggest, be important for understanding the genesis of Greek tragedy out of Dionysiac cult is a possibilty that I can take no further here.

PHILOSOPHY

As for philosophy, there are two ways in which Dionysiac mystic initiation may have contributed to its development. The first derives from the status of mystery-cult as a source of pre-philosophical wisdom. The second, to which I will come in due course, derives from the conception of the *soul* in mystic initiation and in possession trance.

From the early sixth century BC some Greeks began to view the world as a system independent of any personal deity. This is often regarded as a revolution in thought, the beginning of a scientific or philosophical view of the world. Certainly it initiated a conception – of the world without personal gods in control – that in various forms flourished throughout antiquity until the triumph of Christianity, and conflicted with belief in the traditional deities. And yet the myths and rituals of the traditional deities remained so powerful and socially central that it was difficult even for intellectuals to dismiss them altogether. This resulted in various sophisticated attempts to explain some myths as embodying abstract meaning, for instance as allegory. This tendency is especially common for those myths that were told in mystery-cult, for the process of mystic initiation frequently contained the semi-revelation to the initiands of wisdom (what Plutarch called 'telestic wisdom') in an enigmatic form, with the result that myth narrated in mystery-cult attracted allegoric interpretation.

The first mention of Dionysos as embodying an abstract principle is by the philosopher Herakleitos, who lived from the sixth into the fifth century BC. He envisaged the world as structured by the unity of opposites (for instance, he wrote that 'god is day night, winter summer, satiety hunger'). He presents his wisdom in a form derived from the revelation of wisdom in mystery-cult, but attacks mystery-cult as actually practised: he seems to regard his own wisdom as a more abstract and coherent form of mystic wisdom. He maintains, doubtless as an instance of the unity of opposites, that Dionysos and Hades are the same (fragment 15). This is based on the reality that Dionysos, though associated with exuberant life, is also – largely through mystery-cult – associated with the dead (Chapter 5).

The next text (chronologically) to take what seems to be a philosophical view of Dionysos is a passage of Euripides' *Bacchae* in which Teiresias tries to persuade Pentheus that Dionysos is a great god. He maintains that there are 'two first things' among humankind. One is Demeter or Earth, who sustains mortals 'with dry things', and the other is Dionysos, who gave mortals the 'liquid drink' of wine to relieve their sufferings (274–83). Given the role of Pentheus as initiand in *Bacchae* (Chapter 5), it is possible that Teiresias' sermon is influenced by the exposition of myth in Dionysiac mystery-cult. Just as Demeter's introduction of corn was celebrated in her mystery-cult at Eleusis, so Dionysos' introduction of wine might be celebrated in his mystery-cult (Chapter 5).

Mystery-cult might be itself the context of 'philosophical' exposition of the deeper meaning of a mythical narrative, and so would not necessarily exclude the opposition between the dry and the wet in early cosmological and medical theory, or even the sophisticated idea that – as the sophist Prodikos (a contemporary of Euripides) puts it – 'the ancients considered all things that benefit our life gods because of their benefit . . . and for this reason bread was considered to be Demeter and wine Dionysos'. The association of Dionysos not just with the vine but with 'all liquid growth' is asserted centuries later by Plutarch (*Moralia* 365).

DISMEMBERMENT AND THE SOUL

A myth that was more than any other associated with Dionysiac mystery-cult was the story of his dismemberment that we mentioned (as 'Orphic') in Chapter 5. On the prompting of Hera, the primeval deities known as Titans lure away the infant Dionysos by means of a mirror and other objects, and tear him into pieces which they cook and taste. They are punished by being blasted with the thunderbolt of Zeus. Dionysos is then restored to life from his heart, which had been preserved by Athena. The smoke rising from the bodies of the blasted Titans forms a soot, from which is created humankind. This summarises one version of the story, which is told in various versions with differences of detail.

Why is this myth associated with mystic initiation? The fundamental sequence of dismemberment followed by restoration to life belongs to a type found elsewhere expressing the extreme ordeal of imagined death and eventual restoration to life in initiation. Dionysiac (or 'Orphic') mystery-cult had inherited a myth that projected onto Dionysos the imagined bodily death and restoration to life of the initiand. But although this may help to explain the original association of the myth with mystic ritual, this is not how the myth was interpreted by the Greeks themselves. Mystery-cult was a prime context for the transmission of profound or even philosophical wisdom. And so the crude dismemberment myth is *interpreted* as (riddling) allegory.

One such interpretation regards the myth as signifying the harvesting of the grapes in order to make wine, with the new life of Dionysos signifying that the vine then produces new fruit (e.g. Diodorus 3.62.6–7). As suggested in Chapter 5, this interpretation may have been present in the actual practice of drinking wine in the mystery-cult. A more philosophical interpretation – attributed by Plutarch (*Moralia* 389a) to 'theologians' – is that the dismemberment and reunification of Dionysos is a riddling reference to the alternation of multiplicity and unity in the cosmos. Although such alternation is a Stoic idea, its association with the dismemberment myth may owe something to the tendency of mystic wisdom to interpret myth as referring enigmatically to cosmology.

Third, there are various interpretations of the myth as an allegory referring to the human *soul*. This brings us to our second respect in which mystery-cult may have contributed to the development of philosophy.

The Greek word that is generally translated as soul (*psūchē*) refers in Homer to the part of a person that departs the body in swoons or at death, and leads an insubstantial existence in the next world. It has no psychological attributes, plays no part within the living self. In sixth-century texts it has not lost its older meaning but may also refer to the seat of emotions in the living person. The first writer whose *theoretical* statements about the *psūchē* survive is the sixth-century sage Herakleitos. He makes statements about the physical makeup of the *psūchē*, and envisages 'death' for the *psūchē* as a phase of a cycle in which it is transformed into water, water into earth, earth into water, and water back to *psūchē* (fragment 36). The passage of the immortal soul through a cycle of bodily death and birth was a doctrine held in mystery-cult. The 'philosophy' of Herakleitos may be described as a systematised form of mystic doctrine. Some of his statements expressing the unity of opposites (e.g. the one cited earlier in this chapter) bear a remarkable resemblance to the inscriptions on three fifth-century bone plates discovered at Olbia, apparently tokens of having been initiated into mystery-cult (see Chapter 5). One plate has the words 'life death life', 'truth', and 'orphic', another the words 'peace war' over the words 'truth falsehood', and the third has the word '*psūchē*'. All three plates have the name 'Dio<nysos>.'

Given that the sentient *psūchē* in Homer belongs to the next world, and that mystic initiation was a rehearsal of transition to the next world, I suggest that mystery-cult was an important context for the development of the awareness of the sentient *psūchē* in the still-living person. The *psūchē* on the point of death is compared, in a passage of Plutarch, to the experience of mystic initiation (Chapter 5). Mystic initiation, because it was a pre-enactment of death, is experienced by the part of us that survives death, namely the *psūchē*. Moreover, possession trance, to which the mystic initiand might be subjected, implies – whether or not there is 'soul-loss' – the separability of the inner person from the body. The initiates in the next world are described on a funerary gold leaf (Chapter 5) of about 400 BC as *mustai* (initiates), as *bakchoi*, and as *psūchai* (souls). On another gold leaf, of the mid-fourth century BC, it is the *psūchē* that 'leaves the light of the sun' and – it seems – 'became a god'.

We have seen how the liberation effected by mystic ritual, by the telestic madness of Dionysos, is from the agitation or fluttering of the *soul*. It is the soul that becomes the subject of mystic purification and liberation. For Plato the painful fluttering of the soul (at death) is caused by its attachment to the body (*Phaedo* 108ab), within which, according to mystic doctrine, the soul is imprisoned (*Cratylus* 400c; *Phaedo* 62b). Death and purification by philosophy both consist of liberation of the soul from the body, and the verse uttered in mystery-cult stating that Dionysiac initiates (*bakchoi*) are relatively few in number is taken by Plato to be an enigmatic reference to true philosophers (*Phaedo* 67cd, 69cd). How paradoxical that Plato should associate his ideal of the philosophical soul, abstracted from all bodily attractions, with the cult of the luxuriantly corporeal Dionysos! The paradox is possible because the purification of the mystic initiand involved something like the separation of soul from body that occurs in death and in (death-like) possession trance. Euripides' dancing maenads sing of mystic initiation as 'joining the soul (*psūchē*) to the thiasos . . . with holy purifications' (*Bacchae* 75–7). The ritualisation of possession may integrate the individual into the group, notably by means of music.

We can now return to the theme of dismemberment. The dismemberment of Dionysos, being a projection of the fate of the initiand, comes to apply not to the body but – as an allegory – to the soul. The transition from anxiety to joy is envisaged as the transition from mental fragmentation to mental wholeness.

Of this allegorisation the earliest indication is, I think, in the report by Plato (*Laws* 672b) of the story that Dionysos was made mad by Hera, after which, according to another text ('Apollodorus' *Bibliotheca* 3.5.1), he was purified by Rhea, from whom he learnt mystic ritual. Now Hera also incited the *dismemberment* of Dionysos. For the madness she imposed on Dionysos Plato in fact uses the elaborate periphrasis 'was torn apart in the intelligence of his soul' (*diephorēthē tēs psūchēs tēn gnōmēn*). The verb used here is rare, and generally has a *physical* sense: it is for instance used three times in *Bacchae*, of the frenzied tearing apart both of animals (739, 746) and of Pentheus (1210). And so I infer that Plato's periphrasis reflects a mystic interpretation of the dismemberment myth (he mentions the Titans at 701c) as meaning the dismemberment of the soul, i.e. madness. Similarly, *Bacchae* 969–70, in a passage full of mystic allusions, associates physical with psychological fragmentation in the description of Pentheus' mental softness as *truphē*, which derives from *thruptein*, to break into pieces.

In the fifth century AD the neoplatonist philosopher Proclus regarded Plato as following the Orphic myths and interpreting mystic doctrine. In this interpretation, according to Proclus, the dismemberment of Dionysos means that body and soul are divided into many bodies and souls, whereas the undivided heart of Dionysos, from which Athena recomposed his body, is cosmic mind or intellect (*nous*). In neoplatonist philosophy *nous* is undivided; it comprehends in one act of intelligence all intelligible things; and it is merged with but superior to the soul.

This interpretation of the myth is metaphysical. It explains the paradox that the intelligible is a unity shared by separate individuals. In Dionysiac initiation the individual 'merges his/her soul with the thiasos' (*Bacchae* 72–6), just as conversely the loss of Dionysos may leave each member of the thiasos in 'isolated desolation' (*Bacchae* 609). Dionysos may unite the souls of individuals in the thiasos, and he may signify transcendent psychic unity. And just as in the Orphic myth he is king of all the gods when he is dismembered, so he may signify *cosmic* unity (of *nous*). Platonic philosophers do not merge their souls in a Dionysiac thiasos: they seek unity not in ecstatic group consciousness but in the trans-personal unity – abstract and universal – of the rational or intelligible.

Because in neoplatonist philosophy the sage aims to ascend to the transcendent unity of the intelligible, the dismemberment myth also acquires an *ethical* dimension. The analogy, implicit in our passage of Plato's *Laws*, between the physical dismemberment of Dionysos and the distraction of his soul (madness) suggests that the eventual restoration of his reconstituted body to life was envisaged as the restoration of wholeness to the distracted soul. The narrative of fragmentation and (potentially restored) unity is enacted not just in the cosmos but within the individual soul. Proclus, for instance, maintains that our *nous* is Dionysiac, and that to transgress against the nous, to tear apart its undivided nature, is to act like the Titans (*Commentary on Plato's Cratylus* 44d). According to the neoplatonist philosopher Iamblichus it was a Pythagorean maxim that 'one must not pull apart the god within oneself' (*VP* 85, 240).

The fifth-century AD poet Nonnus wrote that Dionysos was looking at his image in a mirror when killed by the Titans (6.172–3). This mythical mirror derives from the mirror used in mystic ritual (Chapter 5). Like the dismemberment, the mirror too is deployed to express philosophical ideas. This remarkable deployment was possible because, whatever precisely the use of the mirror in the ritual, it is likely to have included the idea that the mirror provides access to a mysterious other identity of the initiand. Painted on an Apulian bell-krater in Zurich is a young man (about to be struck by a maenad with a sword) looking at a reflection of himself that is nevertheless of a maenad (i.e. female!). In Euripides a doomed bride laughs at the 'lifeless image of her body' in a mirror (*Medea* 1162). The association of the mirror image with death or with the soul is found in numerous cultures. Apollodorus Grammaticus maintained that souls were 'like images appearing in mirrors' (Stobaeus *Florilegium* 1.49). In the sixth century AD the neoplatonist Olympiodorus wrote that 'Dionysos, when he put his image into the mirror, followed it, and in this way was divided up into the universe.' The dismemberment myth may signify not only the relationship between unity and plurality in the mind, but also the *failure* of our minds to realise unity. It may function like a myth of original sin. Already in the third century AD Plotinus had noted the power of a mirror to 'seize a form', and a few lines later writes that 'the souls of men, having seen their images, like Dionysos (had seen his) in a mirror, became there (i.e. in the images) by leaping from above, but not cut off from their own principle and intellect (*nous*)' (*Enneads* 4.3.12).

Here Plotinus has in mind not just Dionysos looking into a mirror but more specifically the whole story of him being lured – by the sight of his own image in the mirror – to being dismembered by the Titans, as signifying the fall and fragmentation of the soul into material reality. Elsewhere in Plotinus, and in Plato, the idea of an inferior order of reality is expressed as (insubstantial) reflection. Plotinus also refers to the myth of Narcissus – as expressing the misguided pursuit of the beauties of the visible world, which are in fact only a reflection of internal beauty (1.6.8; 5.8.2). And yet not all is lost. Souls are 'not cut off' from their earlier state. We may return towards our original state of psychic unity. The 'longing to be with yourselves, in gathering yourselves together apart from the body' is described by Plotinus as a 'bacchic frenzy' (1.6.5). Plato had mentioned 'sharing in philosophical madness and *bakcheia*': philosophy is imagined as the frenzy of a Dionysiac thiasos (*Symp.* 218b3).

On this kind of interpretation the soul is associated with Dionysos (and with his fatal attraction to his own reflection). But it may, we have seen, act like the Titans in offending against *nous*. This association of the human soul with the disorderly violence of the mythical Titans coheres with the ancient and widespread idea that human beings derive in one way or another from the Titans. And the mythical punishment of the Titans for their transgressions provides for allegorical interpretation an explanation for the inborn sufferings of human souls. In a late version of the Orphic myth humans derive from the soot left by the smoke from the Titans blasted by the thunderbolt of Zeus for their crime against Dionysos. Plutarch associates this crime with the identification of the Titans with what is irrational, violent, and disorderly imprisoned (as punishment) within us (*Moralia* 996bc).

The idea that we may be being punished for the Titans' murder of Dionysos was probably current, albeit secret, at least as early as the fifth century BC. The idea that we – or our *psūchai* – are imprisoned in bodies for an unnamed crime is attributed by Plato to 'those around Orpheus' and to mystery-cult (*Cratylus* 400c; *Phaedo* 62b). On the *Phaedo* passage Plato's fourth-century BC pupil Xenocrates (fragment 20) comments that it is the Titans who are imprisoned within human-kind, and seems to have added a reference to their killing of Dionysos (but this was a perhaps added by the later writer who reports him). The Titans' dismemberment of Dionysos was not their only crime (they also rebelled against the gods), but perhaps it was the unnamed crime mentioned by Plato. He also reports (*Meno* 81ab) that certain 'priests and priestesses' regard the immortal soul as passing through a cycle of 'death' and birth, and quotes a passage of Pindar to the effect that those from whom Persephone (as queen of the underworld) will receive compensation for ancient grief (or consisting in ancient grief) will have their souls (*psūchai*) restored by her to the sun and will be called for the rest of time pure heroes. It has been argued that the 'ancient grief' is Persephone's at the Titans' dismemberment of her son Dionysos, for which the Titans pay compensation by being imprisoned within mankind. This view is consistent with a gold leaf (Chapter 5) containing the words 'say to Persephone that Bakchios himself released you'. Other probable allusions to the myth are in Herodotus (2.42, 61, 132, 170) and Isocrates (11.39).

Do these various interpretations of the myth as about the soul originate in mystery-cult or in philosophy? Plato is explicitly citing mystic doctrine. But in the case of his neoplatonist successors the answer is not so easy. Perhaps the interpretations were contained, in some form, in mystery-cult, if only as doctrine influenced by philosophy. The myth, which once expressed the imagined fate of the Dionysiac initiand, might easily come to be interpreted – from the ambitious perspective characteristic of mystic doctrine – as explaining human suffering as punishment for the dismemberment of Dionysos by the Titans, from whom human beings derive. Because mystic ritual is a pre-enactment of the terrors of death and of subsequent bliss in the next world, it also becomes a means of escape from our sufferings in this world, and so a means of final absolution from the mythical crime (committed by the Titans) that is being punished by our sufferings.

To conclude: within the traditional mystic myth the dismemberment of Dionysos expresses first the imagined bodily experience of the initiand, then his psychological experience, and then the state of soul fragmented in the material world, as well as a transgression (by the Titans) comparable to our 'original sin'. How widespread were these ideas? It is impossible to know. Sepulchral inscriptions with some Dionysiac content are not unusual in the period of the Roman empire, and none of them states or implies that the *soul* has departed from the body for a better place. This suggests that such an idea may have been largely confined to a philosophical elite, or – if more widespread – regarded as mystic doctrine not to be made public.

OVERVIEW

In this chapter Dionysos has vastly expanded the range of his associations. From being a god physically present in wine, ritual, drama, and the underworld, he has now – through the experience of the soul in mystery-cult – acquired a symbolic association with the fate of the human soul. This is in part a symptom of the conservatism and interconnectedness of ancient thought. What we tend to separate, ancient thought – whether mythical or philosophical – tends to see as a whole. The result is a god with something for everybody, well equipped to survive the demise of ancient polytheism.

9

CHRISTIANITY

INTRODUCTION

From our perspective it can seem that Christianity was a sudden revolution, the unpreventable explosion of something entirely new into the world. In fact of course Christianity derived much from Judaism and from Greek religion. And it was established through long-lasting and often violent conflicts, in the course of which it was confronted with rival religious beliefs and practices. One such rival was the cult of Dionysos. As we have seen, the widespread popularity of Dionysos ranged from the simple practices of peasants to the abstract speculations of intellectuals, and he could save mortals from the terrors of death. He was therefore a serious rival to Jesus, whom in some respects he resembled.

DIONYSOS AND THE JEWS

For the great Hellenistic monarchies of western Asia (the Seleucids) and Egypt (the Ptolemies) we have seen that there was no god more important than Dionysos. Occupying a place between these two kingdoms, and at times a prize of warfare between them, was the fertile land of Palestine, homeland of (some of) the Jews.

The relationship of Dionysos to the Jews of Palestine seems to have taken various forms. First, there may well have been direct pressure on the Jews from the Hellenistic monarchs to practise the cult of Dionysos. Much of the evidence for this is from the books named *Maccabees* (after the leader of the revolt of 168/7 BC by traditionalist Jews against Hellenisation under the Seleucids). For instance, it is claimed – perhaps with exaggeration – that under the Seleucid king Antiochus IV the Jews were compelled to wear ivy wreaths and walk in procession in honour of Dionysos (*2 Maccabees* 6.7).

Dionysos was envisaged as a god constantly on the move, a traveller over vast distances – notably in his conquest (like Alexander) of remote eastern lands. As we would expect, there is evidence that the Greek cities in Palestine recognised Dionysos. This is our second category of evidence. For instance he was said to have founded Scythopolis (in Hebrew named Beth-Shean, about 18 miles south-east of Nazareth), where evidence – mainly from the second century AD – has been unearthed for his cult. That the city was once known as Nysa, the place where in myth Dionysos was reared by the nymphs, is mentioned in the first century AD by Pliny the elder. Other places in Palestine produced coins and works of art with Dionysiac themes, but almost all that survives dates from after the first century AD.

This second category of evidence is confined to the Greek cities, which contained numerous people of entirely Greek culture as well as Jews. Our third category of evidence consists of the Jewish use of symbols that suggest potential for convergence with Dionysiac cult (at least in the eyes of non-Jewish writers). As early as the fourth century BC the famous (Jewish) Yehud coin in the British Museum represents a Silenus mask, along with a seated figure who may be Yahweh. Vines were plentiful in Palestine, and frequently represented in Jewish sculptural reliefs. Various Jewish coins represent grapes, vine-leaves, drinking cups, and such like. At the rededication of the temple in 164 BC the Jews – we are told (*2 Maccabees* 10.7) – carried *thyrsoi*, as also did dancing Jewish women at another celebration related in the book of Judith (15.12). At the entrance to Herod's temple there was a great golden vine.

Plutarch devotes several (deliberately fanciful) paragraphs to the Dionysiac nature of Jewish cult (*Moralia* 671c–672c). Tacitus writes that various features of Jewish cult – the music of pipes and drums, ivy crowns, and the golden vine at the temple – give rise to the view that the Jews worship Liber Pater (Dionysos), the conqueror of the East (*Histories* 5.5).

THE NEW TESTAMENT

It is against this background that we turn to the New Testament. Early in the fourth gospel Jesus transforms water into wine at the wedding feast at Cana (2.1–11), on which the fourth gospel comments that Jesus performed this as the first of the 'signs' (miracles) and manifested his glory. Opinion is divided on the relationship of this episode to the miraculous production of wine by Dionysos in numerous rituals and stories (Chapter 2), which include making water seem like wine (Plutarch, *Life of Lysander* 28.4). One view denies any relationship. Another derives the episode (however indirectly) from the Dionysiac stories. A third view (somewhere in between the other two) regards the episode as in some sense a response – at least for some of the hellenised community for whom the gospel was written – to the implicit challenge represented by the cult of Dionysos, a challenge that may conceivably also underly the claim made by Jesus later in the fourth gospel that 'I am the true vine' (15.1). Dionysos too was identified with the vine.

This third view is supported by a myth preserved in the Greek romance by Achilles Tatius, *The Story of Leucippe and Cleitophon* (2.2.1–3), from which we possess a papyrus fragment of the second century AD. It is said that before the invention of wine a Tyrian shepherd was visited by Dionysos, who offered him a cup of wine. The shepherd drank it, and asked the god 'From where do you have this purple water? Where did you find such sweet blood?' Dionysos replied that 'this is water of harvest, this is blood of the grape', and, squeezing some grapes, 'this is the water; this is the spring'. And so on that day – the story concludes – the people of Tyre celebrate a festival of Dionysos. Tyre is about forty miles north of Nazareth. Jesus visited the territories of Sidon (where in Achilles Tatius the story is told) and of Tyre, and people came from both cities to hear him (Matthew 15.21–2; Mark 3.8; 7.24, 31; Luke 6.17).

Other New Testament passages that may have some relation to Dionysos are from the letters of Paul and the *Acts of the Apostles.*

Paul was a hellenised Jew from Tarsus, which according to Strabo (14.5.13), an older contemporary of Paul, was a flourishing centre of Greek education. Paul spread Christianity to the Greeks, and wrote very competent Greek. Tarsus has not been much excavated, but surely contained a cult of Dionysos. A first century AD inscription from Seleucia ad Calycadnum, about eighty miles west of Tarsus, attests the presence there of Dionysiac mystery-cult.

The Pauline letters sometimes contain clusters of terms or ideas that suggest the influence, direct or indirect, of mystery-cult. One instance is the words 'for now we see through a glass darkly, but then we shall see face to face' (1 *Corinthians* 13.12). What the Greek says is, in modern English, 'through a mirror in a riddle'. The image owes something to the Old Testament (*Numbers* 12.8), but this is not enough to explain it. In mystery-cult the transition from the phase of ignorant anxiety to the phase of joyful knowledge might be effected by the use, in the first phase, of riddling language and of the mirror, both of which gave an obscure image of what was subsequently revealed (ancient mirrors were much obscurer than modern). I have mentioned the use of the mirror in Dionysiac mysteries both in the Villa of the Mysteries at Pompeii and (along with the use of riddling language) in *Bacchae* (Chapter 5). Paul is here imagining eschatological transition in terms taken from the transition (itself embodying a kind of death) from ignorance to knowledge in mystery-cult.

Paul in his letters also proclaims a doctrine of baptism 'into the death' of Jesus Christ, of burial with him (through baptism), and of resurrection associated with his resurrection (*Romans* 6.3–6; also e.g. *Romans* 8.11; *Galatians* 2.20; 3.26–7). This doctrine is to be found neither in the Gospels nor in Judaic religion. It has been suggested that it is influenced by one or more of the forms taken by mystery-cult, whether performed for Greek deities such as Dionysos or Demeter or for deities originating from outside the Greek world such as Isis and Attis.

A huge amount of scholarship has been devoted to this controversial issue over many years, and I do not intend to enter the controversy here. Suffice it to say that although we know of no mystery-cult that reproduces exactly the same configuration as the Pauline doctrine, we do find in mystery-cult the ideas of the death and rebirth of the initiand (e.g. Apuleius *Metamorphoses* 11.21), of the sufferings of the deity (e.g. Athenagoras *Supplication* 32.1), of the identification of initiand with deity, and of the initiands' (transition to) salvation depending on their finding – or the return to life of – a deity (e.g. Lactantius *Divine Institutions* 18.7; Firmicus Maternus *On the Error of Profane Religions* 2.9; 22.1–3).

As for Dionysos, the gold leaves (Chapter 5) preserve the mystic formulae 'Hail you who have suffered what you had never suffered before. You became a god instead of a human,' and 'now you died and now you came into being, thrice blessed one, on this day. Tell Persephone that Bakchios himself freed you.' And the mystic myth of the dismemberment of Dionysos and his restoration to life was probably associated with a similar transition for the initiand in the mystic ritual (Chapters 5 and 8). Most strikingly *Bacchae* 576–641 projects the mystic transition, from despair and fear to joy, caused by the reappearance of the deity, who is identified with light. The chorus, despairing at Pentheus' imprisonment of their 'guardian' (whom we know to be Dionysos), the missionary of the new cult, sing to their god Dionysos, who invokes earthquake, thunder, and lightning. Pentheus' house falls to the ground, and the appearance of Dionysos from within brings joy to the chorus, who had fallen to the ground, each one in 'isolated desolation'. The god then describes the strange behaviour of Pentheus failing to bind him within the house.

Details of this behaviour, and of the experience of the chorus, reappear in accounts of mystic initiation, notably in a fragment of Plutarch (178) in which he compares the experience of dying with the experience of mystic initiation: in both passages there are exhausting runnings around, uncompleted journeys through darkness, fear, trembling, sweat, and then light in the darkness. And they also appear in the description, in the *Acts of the Apostles* (16.25–9), of the miraculous liberation from prison at Philippi: the missionaries of the new religion, Paul and Silas, are imprisoned, singing to their god in the darkness of midnight when there is a sudden earthquake, and (as at *Bacchae* 447–8) the doors open and the chains fall away from the prisoners. The gaoler seizes a sword, is reassured by Paul that the prisoners are still there, asks for light, rushes inside, falls trembling at the feet of Paul and Silas, and is converted to Christianity. So too Pentheus seizes a sword, rushes inside into the darkness, and finally collapses, while Dionysos remains calm throughout and reassures Pentheus that he will not escape. But Pentheus – in attacking with his sword the light made by the god in the darkness – expresses his obdurate resistance to being initiated/converted (antithetically to the chorus, and to the gaoler at Philippi).

The *Bacchae* passage is also similar in several respects to the various accounts in Acts of the conversion of Saul on the road to Damascus. Here the persecutor of the new religion is converted (like the gaoler at Philippi, and in contrast to Pentheus). Divine intervention is sudden (*Bacchae* 576, *Acts* 9.3, 16.26). The group hears the voice of the god but does not see him (*Bacchae* 576–95, *Acts* 9.7). To the lightning in *Bacchae* corresponds the description of the light appearing to Saul in terms of lightning (9.3, 22.6). The Dionysiac chorus falls to the ground and Pentheus collapses, and Saul falls to the ground (as does also, at 26.14, the group that accompanies him). The command to rise up, marking the transition, is given by Dionysos to the chorus and by the Lord to Saul. The chorus and Pentheus identify Dionysos with light; Saul saw the Lord, and it has been inferred that 'Saul's companions saw only a formless glare where he himself saw in it the figure of Jesus' (Haenchen).

These similarities are too numerous to be coincidental. How are we to explain them? One possibility is that they derive from knowledge of *Bacchae*. *Bacchae* was indeed well known in this period: for instance, we hear of it being recited in Corinth in the first century AD (Lucian *The Ignorant Book Collector* 19), and the literary knowledge of the author of the Acts is exemplified by his including a verse of the Hellenistic poet Aratus in Paul's sermon on the Areopagus (17.28). Moreover, in one version of the conversion of Saul the Lord says to him 'It is hard for you to kick against the goads' (26.14). This expression occurs nowhere else in the New Testament, but it does occur in early Greek literature, notably when Dionysos says to his persecutor Pentheus 'Do not kick against the goads, a mortal against a god' (*Bacchae* 796). Pentheus and Saul are advised not to resist by the god whose new cult they are vainly persecuting.

This is not to say that the Greek influence on these passages of *Acts* was necessarily merely literary. It is likely, given the continuity of mystery-cult (Chapter 5), that the mystic ritual reflected in *Bacchae* persisted into the first century AD, and possible that it influenced narratives that have been lost but had some influence – perhaps along with *Bacchae* – on the narratives incorporated into *Acts*.

DIONYSOS UNDER CHRISTIANITY

Dionysos, like Jesus, was the son of the divine ruler of the world and a mortal mother, appeared in human form among mortals, was killed and restored to life. Early Christian writers, aware of the similarity between Christianity and mystery-cult, claim that the latter is a diabolical imitation of the former. The first to make such a claim is Justin Martyr (c. AD 100–165), who notes that Dionysos was said to be the son of god, that wine was used in his mysteries, and that he was dismembered and went up to heaven (*Apologies* 1.54).

Clement of Alexandria, who was born in the middle of the second century AD and converted to Christianity, vigorously attacks the pagan mystery-cults, into which he may in his youth have been initiated, but pays them the implicit tribute of claiming that the *true* mystery is to be found in Christianity. Quoting *Bacchae*, he appeals to Pentheus to 'Throw off your headband! Throw off your fawnskin! Be sober! I will show you the word and the mysteries of the word. . . . If you wish, you too be initiated, and you will dance with angels around the unbegotten and imperishable and only true god' (*Proptrepticus* 12).

Christian writing provides evidence for the persistence of Dionysiac cult until well after Christianity became the official religion of the Roman empire. In about AD 340, according to Sozomenos (*History of the Church* 6.25), two Christian clerics in Laodicea were punished for attending some kind of recitation for Dionysos that was only for the initiated. Augustine (AD 354–430) in one of his letters (17.4) criticises public revelry in honour of Dionysos, in which notables participate. A building excavated at Cosa in Tuscany was used for dining by a Bacchic association from some time in the fourth century AD until well on into the fifth, despite the outlawing of paganism in AD 391 by the emperor Theodosius. And as late as AD 691 the Council of the Church in Constantinople prohibited transvestism, the wearing of masks (comic, satyric, or tragic), and the shouting of the name of the 'detested Dionysos' by those who press the grapes or pour the wine into the jars.

The picture drawn from the church fathers is corroborated by the persistence, into late antiquity, of the popularity of visual representations of the cult and myths of Dionysos, for instance on numerous sarcophagi. Textiles decorated with myths of Dionysos were being produced as late as the sixth century AD in Egypt, where, a century earlier, Nonnus had produced (besides a poetic version of the fourth gospel) the last flowering of Dionysiac literature, the *Dionysiaka*, forty-eight books of poetic narrative about the god. The rich tradition of Dionysiac visual art was an influence on early Christian art, notably in representations of the vine, with which both Dionysos and Jesus were identified. The vine is represented in the earliest surviving Christian art, in the catacombs, and a fine example from the fourth century AD is provided by the Christian mosaics, representing vine tendrils and scenes of the vintage, on the vault of the Mausoleum of Constantia (daughter of the Emperor Constantine) in Rome, subsequently called the church of Santa Costanza.

Wine was imagined as the blood of Dionysos (Chapter 5), and of Jesus. The association of the killing of the god with the crushing of the grapes (for wine-making), that in Chapters 5 and 8 we noted as an allegorical interpretation of the mystic myth of the dismemberment and return to life of Dionysos, appears in Christian form in Clement's characterisation of Jesus as 'the great grape-cluster, the word crushed for our sake' (*Paedagogus* II 19.3), as well as in Romanos' second *Hymn on the Nativity* (sixth century AD), in which Mary responds to her son's prediction of his crucifixion with the words 'O my grapevine (*botrus*), may they not squeeze you out.' Jesus responds by saying that his resurrection will bring new life and renewal to the earth. From the same period a chalice from Antioch shows Jesus and other figures surrounded by vines. In the *Christus Patiens*, a Byzantine cento (poem made up of verses from other sources) that may be as late as the twelfth century AD, the lament of Mary for Christ is composed in part of verses from the (lost) lament of Agaue for Dionysos in *Bacchae*.

It has been suggested that certain ancient representations of Jesus as youthful, beardless, long-haired, and effeminate were influenced by similar representations of Dionysos. But the most striking example of a visual representation of Dionysiac myth that may seem to converge with Christian conceptions is a mosaic scene (one of a series) discovered in 1983 in the 'House of Aion' in Paphos in Cyprus (Figure 6). All the figures are identified by name. The seated god Hermes is about to hand the infant Dionysos to the aged silen 'Tropheus' ('rearer' or 'educator'), while on the left of the scene nymphs prepare his first bath. The names of Hermes' companions – 'Ambrosia', 'Nektar' (personifications of the food and drink of immortals), and 'Theogonia' (Birth of the Gods) – emphasise the divinity of the child, who is the solemn focus of all attention. The bending figure of the approaching Tropheus, and the veiling of Hermes' hands by part of his cloak, resemble contemporary images that derive from the ceremonial of the imperial court. We are reminded of the Orphic tradition in which Zeus sets his son Dionysos on the royal throne and makes him king of all the gods. Although the mosaic may seem to resemble the Christian nativity, there is in fact no hard evidence for supposing specific influence from or on Christianity. However, it may be relevant that the mosaic dates from a time, about the middle of the fourth century, when ancient polytheism was being reshaped in response to the dominant appeal of the Christian universal saviour.

In general, similarity between deities in the ancient Mediterranean area was a factor making for the ancient and ubiquitous process of *syncretism* – the association, assimilation, or identification of deities (and their cults) with each other. Other factors were contact and conquest. Already in the fifth century BC Dionysos is equated by Herodotus (2.144) with the Egyptian Osiris, and in *Bacchae* (79) he is associated with the orgiastic cult of the Anatolian goddess Kybele. The conquests of Alexander vastly extended the scope for the syncretism of Greek with eastern deities, and the process developed unabated during the rise of Christianity. Among the factors making for the susceptibility of Dionysos and his enthusiastic cult to syncretism were their imagined foreign origin (e.g. *Bacchae* 1–20) and the ubiquity of the vine. Dionysos becomes closely associated, or identified, with (among others) Serapis, Dysares, Attis, Sabazios, Mithras, and Hekate, as well as – in Italy – the Roman Liber and the Etruscan Fufluns. In the late pagan attempt to counter Christianity by systematising

Figure 6 Mosaic from the 'House of Aion' in Paphos.

Source: R. Sheridan/Ancient Art & Architecture Collection Ltd.

polytheism, Dionysos is associated – and even (along with other deities) identified – with the Sun.

Christianity, on the other hand, on the whole protected itself from such syncretism, albeit in part by incorporating into itself elements of other religions. Any similarities or mutual influence – in the symbolic structure of ritual or belief – between mystery-cult and Christianity should not blind us to the profound difference in their ethics and organisation. Unlike the (generally nameless) initiates of Dionysos (or of Mithras, etc.), early 'Christians' were organised in regulated self-reproducing communities. The specific identity of the church was thereby preserved, and this was a factor in the eventually complete victory of Christianity over pagan mystery-cult.

OVERVIEW

The Asian conquests of Alexander had spread Hellenism, which included the cult of Dionysos, over numerous subject peoples. One such people were the Jews, whose sense of national identity made them fiercely hostile to Dionysos, not least because of his seductiveness in a vine-growing land. Christianity, an offshoot of Judaism in a Hellenised world, triumphed by simultaneously adapting to that world and nevertheless preserving its own organisational specificity. In doing so, it had to combat the rival appeal of Dionysos (as well as of other cults) without being entirely immune to his influence.

DIONYSOS AFTERWARDS

10

AFTER ANTIQUITY

INTRODUCTION

For the ancient Greeks the gods were a fundamental system for organising experience (belief) and controlling the world (cult). From the European renaissance onwards there have been periods in which the Greek gods have been revived to the extent of being used, by some intellectuals, as the best way of designating and expressing a fundamental aspect of experience, albeit without on the whole inspiring the kind of belief that produces cult. The number of deities revived in this way has never been great, and the most prominent among them has been Dionysos. In this chapter I will focus on a few appearances of the Dionysiac, in various genres, selected mainly from the two most striking phases of this revival, Renaissance Italy and nineteenth-century Germany.

RENAISSANCE ITALY

In antiquity Dionysos appeared with his lover Ariadne in a variety of contexts: in a chariot together in Attic vase-painting, in the tableau at the symposium described by Xenophon (Chapter 7), in the Villa of the Mysteries at Pompeii (Chapter 5), as a bridal couple on tombs, and so on. In the year 1490 Lorenzo ('Il Magnifico') de' Medici wrote a song of the kind designed to accompany mythological floats in the Florentine Carnival procession. It begins thus.

Quant' è bella giovinezza	How beautiful is youth
che si fugge tuttavia:	that ever flees away.
Chi vuol esser lieto sia,	Whoever wants to be joyful, should be.
Di doman non c' è certezza.	Of tomorrow there is no certainty.
Quest' è Bacco e Arianna,	Here are Bacchus and Ariadne
Belli, e l'un dell'altro ardenti:	beautiful, and aflame for each other:
Perché 'l tempo fugge e inganna,	because time flies and deceives us,
sempre insieme stan contenti.	they are always happy in togetherness.

There follows a description of nymphs, satyrs, and Silenus, and then, bringing up the rear, Midas: 'all that he touches turns to gold; and what is the point of having wealth if it does not make him happy?'. This, the main negative note in the song, serves to particularise the principle of living in the moment by opposing it to the deferment inherent in money. The principle, thus particularised, was I believe more central to the ancient Dionysiac than Lorenzo himself may have known (Chapter 11). It is at any rate significant that for Lorenzo Bacchus is not the merely disreputable hedonist that he often is in the middle ages – for example exactly a century earlier in the *Confessio Amantis* by John Gower.

The principle that 'one must live today, for to live tomorrow is to live never' had in 1474 been urged in a letter to Lorenzo by none other than the pioneer of Renaissance Platonism, Marsilio Ficino (with *intellectual* pleasure in mind). Two years after Lorenzo wrote his song, Ficino completed his translation of the *Mystical Theology* by 'Dionysius the Areopagite' (sixth century AD), whom he calls a 'Platonist Christian'. In the Preface Ficino writes that

> ancient theologians and Platonists regarded the spirit of the god Dionysus as the ecstasy and abandon of separated minds, when – in part through inborn love, in part by the instigation of the god – having moved beyond the natural limits of intelligence, they are miraculously transformed into the beloved god: where, as if inebriated by a certain new drink of nectar and by immense joy they are – so to speak – in a bacchic frenzy (*debacchantur*).

Ficino goes on to detect this Dionysiac spirit in the appropriately named Dionysius, and to maintain that in order to understand his profound meanings we too require 'divine fury'.

In his book on Love (1484) Ficino had claimed that four kinds of divine madness perform four successive functions in the ascent of the soul, with the Dionysiac kind (the second phase) reducing – through ritual – the multiplicity of the soul to the intellect alone. The blessings of the four kinds of divine madness are taken from Plato's *Phaedrus*, and there may also be influence from the passage of Plotinus in which 'gathering yourselves together apart from the body' is described as a Dionysiac frenzy (Chapter 8). But in the passage I have cited from his Preface of 1492 Ficino's conception of Dionysiac frenzy is different: it is the mental state that by going *beyond* mere intelligence obtains ecstatic access to profound meanings and to the divine. There is influence here from a doctrine of Plotinus in which

> the Intellect has one power for thinking, by which it sees the things in itself, and the other by which it sees things above itself by a certain intuition . . . this (the latter) is Intellect in love, when drunk with nectar it is out of its mind; then it falls in love, simplified into happiness by the fullness; and it is better for it to be drunk like this than to be sober (*Enneads* 6.7.35).

In his incomplete Commentary (section 10) on Plato's *Phaedrus*, published in 1496 but written earlier, Ficino states that Dionysos 'brings it to pass that minds seem to go beyond their boundaries, as it were, in seeing and also in loving', and 'presides over generation and regeneration'. Ficino's Dionysiac gives identity to the (vaguely sensed) ecstasy of a higher understanding beyond the reach of mere intelligence.

In the period in which Ficino was engaged on these studies, a boy aged 15 was taken by Lorenzo Medici into his household. This was Michelangelo (1475–1564). From the brilliant circle of the Medici the boy received various influences, including – from Ficino, directly or indirectly – a lasting interest in Platonism. In 1496 Michelangelo left Florence for Rome. Here his first sculpture was of Bacchus, a pioneering masterpiece in the ancient style, now in the Bargello museum in Florence. The god stands in the precarious balance of the drunk, holding a cup of wine.

But this is not just an image of vulgar drunkenness. First, he has the charisma of a god. Second, he holds in his left hand, by his left thigh, an animal skin (of a leopard, it seems) containing a bunch of grapes which a smiling little satyr is putting to his mouth. The head of the flayed animal droops between the satyr's goat feet. What is the significance of the animal skin? Maenads were imagined as tearing animals apart. In a later poem Michelangelo imagines the shedding of his 'hairy skin' – so as to cover the living body of his beloved – as the transformation of identity through death. Flaying may be taken to express the painful removal of the outer man from the spirit, as in the famous prayer, in Dante's *Paradiso* (1.19–21), to Apollo: 'enter my breast and infuse your spirit, as when you drew Marsyas from the sheath of his limbs'. Ficino had distinguished two kinds of drunkenness: one of them is vulgar, but by means of the other the mind moves outside and above itself, forgets mortal afflictions, and enters the sphere of the divine (*Opera Omnia* 1399). Whatever the relevance or otherwise of these and other such considerations, the eating of the grapes from the skin of the flayed animal held by the drunken god embodies a striking *opposition*, between immortal sensual joy and painful animal death. It is an opposition that is, in a different form, found also – whether Michelangelo knew it or not – in the ancient mystery-cult of the god.

After Lorenzo's song, Ficino's theology, and Michelangelo's sculpture, my final item from the Italian Renaissance is a painting. In 1523 Titian delivered to Alfonso d'Este , for the Studio in his castle at Ferrara, a painting that is now in the National Gallery in London, *Bacchus and Ariadne* (Figure 7). This was one of various thematically interrelated paintings with which Alfonso decorated his Studio. Its theme is the appearance of Bacchus to Ariadne on the island of Naxos, after her abandonment by Theseus. Bacchus, leaping from his chariot, startles Ariadne, who stands with her back to the viewer. He is accompanied by his retinue, and his chariot is pulled by what seem to be cheetahs.

The main literary source for this picture is the narrative in Ovid's *Ars Amatoria* (1.525–64), in which Ariadne wanders on the shore, barefoot, with beltless tunic and yellow hair unbound. She laments the departure of Theseus. Then the thiasos arrives to the sound of cymbals and drums. There are maenads, satyrs, and Silenus riding on an ass. Bacchus himself rides on a chariot drawn by tigers: 'Three times she tried to flee, and three times she was held back by fear.' The god

Figure 7 Bacchus and Ariadne, Titian.

Source: Courtesy of the National Gallery.

promises her marriage, and that she will be the constellation Corona (Crown). Then, 'lest she fear the tigers, he leaps down from the chariot'.

Almost all these details can be found in the painting. The posture of Ariadne seems to me best explained by her abortive attempts to flee, rather than by (as has been suggested) the detail, found in another version, that Dionysus comes on Ariadne 'having followed her from behind' as she walks lamenting on the beach (Ovid *Fasti* 3.508). This does not mean that there is only one literary source for the picture, for it reflects also the description by Catullus (64.257–65) of some members of Bacchus' retinue (as he seeks Ariadne) 'throwing around the limbs of a dismembered steer' and others 'girding themselves with twisting serpents'. But neither in Catullus nor anywhere in Ovid do we have exotic *cheetahs* drawing the chariot. As for Bacchus' promise of transformation into Corona, in the painting the immortal constellation is already there, in the form of eight stars in its top left hand corner. The painting embodies the transition from despairing isolation to immortality through the sudden epiphany of divine love, and is thereby comparable in its solemnity to the epiphany of Dionysos to Ariadne sculpted – with its mystic implication of immortality – on ancient tombs.

NINETEENTH-CENTURY GERMANY

We now move forward three centuries and to Germany, where I will focus mainly on two figures, the poet Friedrich Hölderlin (1770–1843) and the classical scholar and philosopher Friedrich Nietzsche (1844–1900).

Hölderlin sometimes evokes the Dionysiac even where Dionysos himself is not mentioned, as for instance when he writes in his novel *Hyperion* of 'the moments of liberation, when the divine bursts open the prison, . . . when it is for us as if the unchained spirit . . . returns to the halls of the sun'. But I focus on explicit references to Dionysos from Hölderlin's poetic output in the years from 1797 to 1800. A poem about poetry ('An unser grosse Dichter') begins (translations are my own)

> The banks of Ganges heard the joyful god's
> triumph, when all-conquering from Indus
> the young Bacchus came, with holy
> wine from sleep the peoples rousing.

Here the ancient fantasy of the triumphal return of Dionysos from India (Chapter 3) expresses for Hölderlin what it never expresses in antiquity: the power of poetry to effect universal social transformation.

In another poem ('Wie wenn am Feiertage . . .') poetic inspiration is expressed by the myth of Semele wishing to see Zeus in person and so being struck by his lightning that caused her to give birth to Dionysos. 'And hence it is that the sons of earth drink heavenly fire without danger,' and poets should 'grasp the father's ray and offer to the people the heavenly gift wrapped in song.'

In the poem entitled *Brot und Wein* Hölderlin is concerned with the withdrawal of the gods from our world. Prominent among the absent gods, and yet in a sense present, is Dionysos. From the pines and grapes on Mt. Kithairon, beneath which the rivers of Thebes roar, 'comes *der kommende Gott* (the god who comes) and points back to them'. On their withdrawal the gods left here wine (the gift of the 'thundering god') and bread as tokens of their eventual return. That is why, continues Hölderlin, we think of the Heavenly ones, who once were here and will return. And that is why singers praise Dionysos, and state that he reconciles day with night and leads the stars eternally upwards and downwards, and is always glad, like the leaves of the evergreen pine that he loves, and like the crown of ivy, since it lasts and brings the trace of the departed gods down to the godless in their gloom. Meanwhile, until the return of the gods, poets are like 'the holy priests of the wine god, travelling from country to country in holy night'.

Bread and wine suggest the eucharist. As the poem ends Dionysos and Christ are assimilated to each other: 'but meanwhile' (i.e. until the final epiphany) 'as torchbearer the son of the Highest, the Syrian, comes down among the shadows. Blissful wise men see it; a smile is lit up from the imprisoned soul.' In the background are the similarities between Dionysos and Christ that we described in Chapter 9, and in the foreground the 'son of the highest, the Syrian' suggests Christ but also Dionysos, for Dionysos too comes from Asia – notably in *Bacchae*, in which moreover he is described as 'holding up the flame of the pine torch, like smoke of Syrian frankincense . . .' (144–6).

Finally, in an elegy entitled 'Stuttgart' Hölderlin writes of a celebration of the vintage:

> Only one thing matters for the day, the fatherland, and into the sacrifice's
> festive flame everybody throws his own.
> That is why the communal god rustling like wind around us crowns our hair,
> And the wine dissolves our selfish sense like pearls.

The 'communal god (*der gemeinsame Gott*)' here is Bacchus, whom elsewhere Hölderlin calls *gemeingeist* (communal spirit).

Understanding this Dionysiac imagery in the poetry of Hölderlin's youth requires us to be aware both of his reaction against the restrictive Protestant establishments in which he was educated and of his sympathy with the democratic ideals of the French Revolution. He spent his youth in an area of Germany which was in these years subject to incursions over the Rhine by the French revolutionary army. Several revolutionaries from the circle to which Hölderlin belonged were in 1800 imprisoned by the Duke of Württemberg, who shortly afterwards was forced by French military success to release them. In antiquity Dionysos was associated with sudden ecstasy and with communality, and the charisma of his triumphal return from India (Chapter 3) may have seemed to imply the universal victory of Hellenism. Hölderlin develops these associations to express political excitement in the decade after the French Revolution.

The Dionysiac in Hölderlin perpetuates various characteristics of the ancient Dionysos. First, there is his ancient association with poetry and with the frenzy in which poetry is produced. Second, there are the contradictions that qualify him to mediate between mortals and the gods, who for Hölderlin are absent. Son of a god, his entry into life is the death of his mortal mother. He departs and returns, may be present in e.g. mask or ivy or vine, may go unnoticed in human form, and so even his absence may seem to imply his presence. Third, there is his cosmic significance. In Sophokles' *Antigone*, for instance, he is called 'chorus-leader of the stars'. Fourth, there is his inspiration of communal feeling. In Hölderlin these four characteristics are transformed and fused to express his vision of the interrelation of poetic ecstasy, the return of the departed gods, and the universal social transformation associated with the French Revolution.

Hölderlin was claimed by Friedrich Nietzsche as his favourite poet. In 1872 Nietzsche in *The Birth of Tragedy* (§1) produced the following evocation of the epiphany of Dionysos:

> Under the spell of the Dionysiac not only is the bond between one human being and another recreated, but also Nature – alienated, hostile or subjugated – celebrates again her festival of reconciliation with her lost son, humankind. Of her

own accord the earth offers her gifts, and peacefully the beasts of prey approach from the rocks and the desert. With flowers and crowns is the waggon of Dionysos covered: under his yoke stride panthers and tigers. Transform Beethoven's *Hymn to Joy* into a painting and fully exercise your imagination, when the millions sink awestruck into the dust: then can you approach the Dionysiac. Now is the slave a free man, now all the rigid, hostile boundaries that necessity, caprice, or 'impudent fashion' have established between human beings are broken. Now, with the gospel of world harmony, everybody feels not just united, reconciled, fused with his neighbour, but as one with him, as if the veil of *māyā* had been torn and was now only fluttering in tatters around the mysterious primordial unity. In singing and dancing humanity expresses itself as member of a higher community . . . Just as now the animals speak and the earth gives milk and honey, so something supernatural sounds from him too: he feels himself as a god. . . .

In this extract we recognise features of the Dionysos of antiquity: his triumphal procession (Chapter 4), the unity of humankind with nature (Chapter 2), the miraculous issue of milk and honey from the earth (Chapter 4), human communality (Chapter 3), and the dissolution of boundaries – between slave and free man, between human and animal, between human and god. But the idea of *māyā* introduces a different note. It is a Sanskrit word meaning illusion or the power of magic, and was used in the Indian Vedanta of the power of the world, with its apparent multiplicity, to conceal (veil) the unity of the individual with Brahma (absolute soul).

This idea had been adopted by the philosopher Schopenhauer (1788–1860), whom Nietzsche has a little earlier cited as in effect associating the veil of *māyā* with the *principium individuationis*. By this 'principle of individuation' Schopenhauer meant the principle by which man perceives the world – through the media of space, time and causality – as a multiplicity of individual appearances. Nietzsche associates the Dionysiac with intoxication ('Rausch'), and with the joyful ecstasy that arises from the collapse of the *principium individuationis*, and with access to the primordial oneness of all things. This resembles ideas associated with the ancient Dionysos – the dissolution of the boundaries enclosing the individual and the concealed unity of everything intelligible (Chapters 5 and 8). Moreover, rather as in antiquity a metaphysical interpretation of the dismemberment and reunification of Dionysos was associated with ancient mystery-cult (Chapter 8), so too Nietzsche (§10) associates not only the dismemberment of Dionysos with the sufferings of individuation but also the joyful celebration of his rebirth in mystery-cult with the 'end of individuation'. But the ancient Dionysiac is (in §1) developed by Nietzsche in a rather different metaphysical direction influenced indirectly by Indian philosophy. Nietzsche even goes so far as to write of the 'foundation of all existence, the Dionysiac substratum (*Untergrund*) of the world' (§25).

Nietzsche adds that this *Dionysiac* substratum of the world can enter the consciousness of the individual only in so far as it can be overcome by the *Apolline* power of transfiguration (*Verklärungskraft*). The Dionysiac is not just a metaphysical principle but also an 'art drive' (*Kunsttrieb*). The Dionysiac and the Apolline are antithetical art drives, the former associated with intoxication (and expressed especially in music), the latter with dreaming and with the illusion of individuation (and expressed especially in sculpture). They generally run parallel – and antagonistically – to each other, but 'by a metaphysical miracle' of the Greek will are combined to produce Attic tragedy.

The Dionysiac aspect of tragedy is manifest especially in the satyrs that Nietzsche supposes to have constituted the chorus of primitive tragedy (compare Chapter 7), and it is from this chorus that the action of tragedy emerges as a vision that is both Dionysiac and Apolline. The satyrs, divine followers of Dionysos, combine animality with wisdom. They are 'proclaimers of wisdom from the inner heart of nature'. In their presence, according to Nietzsche, the audience has a consoling sense of unity with nature. More specifically, they represent nature *as opposed to culture* (§7).

The Greek man of culture (*Kulturmensch*) felt himself nullified in the presence of the chorus of satyrs: and this is the most immediate effect of Dionysiac tragedy, that the state and society, and generally the divisions between human beings, yield to an overwhelming feeling of unity that goes back to the heart of nature. The metaphysical comfort that . . every true tragedy leaves us with, that fundamentally life is, despite all the changes of appearances, indestructibly powerful and pleasurable, this comfort appears clearly embodied as the chorus of satyrs, as the chorus of natural beings (*Naturwesen*), who live as if ineradicably behind all civilisation and remain eternally the same despite all the changes of generations and of the history of peoples.

The 'truth of nature' (*Naturwahrheit*), embodied in the satyr, contrasts with the 'lie of culture', (*Kulturlüge*), and this contrast is 'similar' to that between the eternal core of things (the thing in itself) and the whole world of appearances (§8). And so – to summarise – the dissolution of limits (between humanity and nature, and between one human being and another) combines with nature (as opposed to culture) and with metaphysical permanence (as opposed to changing appearances), and this combination is embodied in the Dionysiac chorus of satyrs that constitutes primitive tragedy.

For at least a century before Nietzsche wrote *The Birth of Tragedy* numerous German intellectuals – far more than in England or France – had pondered the Dionysiac not as mere matter for scholarship but as a *principle* that retains significance for the contemporary world. The antithesis between Dionysos and Apollo goes back in fact to antiquity: Plutarch contrasted the music of Dionysos with that of Apollo, and extended the contrast to a more general one between the 'uniformity, orderliness, and unmixed seriousness' of Apollo as depicted by artists and 'a certain mixed playfulness, aggressiveness, seriousness, and frenzy' in their depictions of Dionysos (*Moralia* 389b). The Apolline and the Dionysiac were elaborated as contrasting ideal types of beauty by the art historian Winckelmann (1717–68), as contrasting creative principles by the philosopher Schelling (1775–1854), and by the jurist and anthropologist Bachofen (1815–87) as contrasting principles that include sexuality, gender, spirituality, and social organisation. Bachofen also maintained that whereas politics creates barriers between individuals, Dionysos removes them and 'leads everything back to unity' (*Discourse Concerning the Tomb Symbolism of the Ancients* (1859)).

This selection of examples briefly indicates that the use made of the Dionysiac in *The Birth of Tragedy* is less original than may at first appear. The originality that it does have consists not so much in any single one of its elements as in their combination into a persuasive whole. This persuasiveness has, despite the criticisms of its scholarship made ever since its first appearance, ensured it considerable and enduring influence.

Finally, one weakness of Nietzsche's account deserves emphasis. He dismisses the view that the tragic chorus (in the *orchestra*) represents the people as opposed to the royal personages (on the stage), and goes so far as to state that 'from the purely religious origins [of tragedy] the whole opposition between people and prince, and generally the entire politico-social sphere, is excluded' (§7). This expresses Nietzsche's distaste for the 'politico-social sphere' of his own time, and seems directed against the kind of interpretation of tragedy represented earlier by Hegel (1770–1831). On Nietzsche the French revolution no longer has the influence that it had on so many earlier German thinkers, including Hölderlin. For him the Dionysiac unity of humankind has no political significance.

Still less were the ideas of the French revolution influential in England. In the 'Study of Dionysus' by the eclectic English aesthete Walter Pater (1839–94) there is just one footnote, which, because it is the only one, seems designed to state something that would have disturbed the serene flow of the main text and yet had to be stated. On the fact that 'even the slaves have their holiday' the footnote adds 'there were some who suspected Dionysos of a secret democratic interest. Though indeed he was liberator only of men's hearts.' Pater, like Nietzsche, goes out of his way to dismiss the possibility of a political dimension to Dionysos.

Finally, the ahistorical Nietzschean Dionysos lived on into the twentieth century. The French philosopher Gilles Deleuze, in the conclusion to his *Différence et Répétition* (1968), associates the 'greatest effort of philosophy' with 'causing a little of Dionysus' blood to flow in the organic veins of Apollo'. In his *The Philosophical Discourse of Modernity* (German original 1985) Jürgen Habermas argues that the 'Dionysiac messianism' of Nietzsche is inherited by Martin Heidegger: 'Nietzsche had entrusted the overcoming of nihilism to the aesthetically revived Dionysiac myth. Heidegger projects this Dionysian happening onto the screen of a critique of metaphysics, which thereby takes on a world-historical significance. Now it is Being that has withdrawn itself from beings . . .'. In contrast to such hyperabstractions, in the twenty-first century the work of uncovering the embeddedness of the Dionysiac in the life of antiquity has gathered pace.

OVERVIEW

We have brought the argument of this book back to its starting point, the present day. In doing so we have concentrated on the two European cultures in which Dionysos most flourished as a symbol. It is perhaps not a coincidence that they were also two of the most intellectually creative periods in European history: Italy in the Renaissance and Germany in the nineteenth century.

11

DIONYSOS AND MONEY,
THEN AND NOW

One aspect of the development of humankind has been (uneven) progression towards the alienation of individuals from nature and from each other. The ancient Greeks, who in their earliest recorded history were experiencing this progression in a rapid form, were thereby left with a sense of loss, of absence. But absence implies the possibility of presence, and the absence and presence of the transcendent power that unites us with nature and with each other is projected onto an imagined person, Dionysos. Dionysos was not invented out of nothing, but the result of continuous adaptation of deity to evolving needs. In this he is like other deities, but more likely than they are to embody what has been lost.

In particular, he retains an association with plants and animals that may once have been shared by other major gods. Besides transforming himself and mortals into various animals, he is identified with the embodiment in nature of our transformability, the plant that dissolves the boundaries of the individual mind, the vine (Chapter 2). Dionysiac ecstasy, whether or not sustained by wine, dissolves the identity of the individual so as to enhance the sense of belonging to a group, in particular to the thiasos, the cohesive sacred band – probably of prehistoric origin – that imagines itself to be the companions of the god. Similar communal feeling may also be experienced by the polis as a whole. Hence the political significance of the Dionysiac thiasos and of the polis festival of Dionysos (Chapter 3).

Ritually induced subjective transformation of this kind, the sudden overpowering of the individual self, may seem to require the arrival of an external power, and this power is embodied in the epiphany of the god (Chapter 4). It is above all the ritual of mystic initiation that overpowers the isolated individual, and by dissolving fundamental boundaries – notably between animal and human, human and divine, male and female, living and dead – transforms the initiand into his or her *opposite*. Or rather, because the initiand cannot but also retain his or her previous identity, Dionysos *unites* the opposites. The mystic transition is also a pre-enactment of death – transforming the initiand into a member of Dionysos' thiasos in this world and the next (Chapter 5). And so the mystic Dionysos both ensures his adherents happiness in the next world, and is himself – as a model for their ritual death – dismembered and restored to life (Chapter 6).

The Dionysiac transformation of identity contributed furthermore to the momentous Greek developments of drama and of philosophy. An important factor in the genesis of tragedy was Dionysiac mystery-cult, and in particular two basic features of it: the transformation of identity, and the epiphanically resolved tension between the (suffering) isolated individual and the (choral) thiasos (Chapter 7). The Platonic opposition between perishable body and imperishable soul owes something to the prefiguration in mystic ritual of the separation of the soul from the body at death. Moreover the transforming presence of Dionysos may – as in the possession cults of our time – occupy the interior of his adherent, thereby contributing to the idea of an opposition between interior (soul) and body, as well as to the Neoplatonic allegorisation of Dionysos as the soul. The abstraction of Dionysos begins in antiquity (Chapter 8).

Chapters 2 to 8 documented the power of Dionysos, in his various manifestations, to transform individual identity. Chapter 9 concerned the elimination of this power by the Christian church, and Chapter 10 gave some examples of the subsequent re-emergence in Europe of respect for the irreducible specificity of the joyful Dionysiac transformation.

The abstractions identified with the Dionysiac in the modern era (Chapter 1) are not without value, but only provided that they are grounded in ancient practice and belief, historicised. For instance the association of Dionysos with the dissolution of boundaries or with the unity of opposites was not the embodiment of a metaphysical principle but rather was shaped by its specific contexts of enactment, notably the ritual of mystic initiation. Furthermore, in order to understand the Dionysiac we must also historicise its opponent: the *individual* whose boundaries are by Dionysos dissolved.

We see ancient Greek individualism through the filter of our own. Our individualism is consumerist. Each of us is to some extent constructed as an individual by virtue of his or her power of expenditure. Money buys almost everything (not least political power), most interpersonal contacts are mediated by money, people create their lives and identities by the use of money. In our 'democratic' consumerist societies we undergo invisible ideological pressure to imagine ourselves as sovereign self-identical individuals making free political and consumer choices, in complete isolation from nature. The moral, emotional, and intellectual abyss by which such a self-image must be surrounded creates the need for a transcendent power, whether for a narrow-minded god to reinforce the boundaries of the self or for a less defined power that threatens to dissolve them – a power that we may construct and name in various ways.

Did Greek individualism of the archaic and classical eras have – despite the obvious differences – anything in common with ours? I believe that it did. The first society in history to be pervaded (and so transformed) by the use of *money* was that of the advanced Greek city-states of the sixth century BC (largely through the invention of coinage). This era has been seen as a period of the 'growing emanicipation of the individual from the old family solidarity' (E. R. Dodds).

I suggest that this development occurs in part as a result of the isolating effect of monetisation. This brave new world of money is a very recent development in the experience of the human species, and the first poetic genre to be created in it was tragedy, which centres around an unprecedented individual known also from historiography and philosophy: the *tyrant*, isolated from the gods and even from his own kin, obsessed with money, a transgressor against the ancient moral codes of reciprocity, the sacred, and kinship. Because money embodies interpersonal power, and lends itself to individual possession, it promotes an unprecedented degree of individual autonomy, and so seems to loosen its possessor from the old moral codes, even from dependence on kin and gods. The tyrant is the new individual, the man of money, writ large. In the Dionysiac genre of tragedy the isolated autocrat is generally destroyed, whereas his opposite, the anonymous choral collective, uphold traditional morality and survive.

A fine example (representing the prototype) of this pattern is the only tragedy that survives on a Dionysiac theme, *Bacchae*. Moreover, the play is pervaded by the contrast between the obstinate isolation of the tyrannical Pentheus (from kin, deity, and everybody else) and the solidarity of the Dionysiac chorus (Chapter 3). Pentheus imagines even the Dionysiac cult in terms of money: he supposes Teiresias' adoption of the new cult to be for monetary gain (257), and at the pivot of the action, the very point at which he is somehow transformed from an obstinately aggressive enemy of the new Dionysiac cult into docile fascination with it, he is asked whether he would like to see the maenads on the mountainside, and replies that he would give much money to do so (811–2). Even the forbidden Dionysiac sight is seen in terms of money. In their next song Dionysos' thiasos ask what is best for mortals, and answer that it has to be eternal, and so is not power over enemies. Moreover, competition for power and wealth is uncertain, in contrast to the eternal happiness brought to every day by mystic initiation (897–912).

The same contrast, between the man of money and initiation into the Dionysiac thiasos, is found elsewhere, in particular in the myth of Midas, which is at least as old as the sixth century BC. Midas captured Silenos, the wise companion of Dionysos, and asked him what is best for humankind. Silenos replied by calling Midas 'ephemeral', and revealed that for humankind it is best never to have been born, and second best to die as soon as possible. Silenos also spoke of 'natural and ancient things'. As a reward for releasing Silenos Midas was offered by Dionysos (or Silenos) the fulfilment of any wish, and chose the power to transform all things by his touch into gold.

This means that Midas' own answer to his question about what is best for humankind is *money*. Midas' touch is the reaction of the Greek mythical imagination to the new (unknown in Homer) and astonishing power of precious metal as universal equivalent: everything can now be valued in money. Midas' subsequent regret, when even his food turns to gold, expresses the negative aspect of this development: absorption in happiness in the abstract (money) can become incapacity for happiness in the concrete. In one version of the myth Midas is initiated into the Dionysiac or Orphic mysteries, recognizes Silenos as a fellow-member of the thiasos, is saved from his own monetary power by Dionysos, and thereafter dwells in the wild, worshipping Pan.

Why is the antithesis to Midas represented by Silenos? Whereas Midas is the new man of money, Silenos is associated with what is 'natural' and 'ancient', to nature as yet unmediated by money. The Dionysiac thiasos transcends separate households but is nevertheless – in its intimate solidarity – distinct from the polis, and may represent the persistence of a social and cultic unit much more ancient than the polis. Whereas the abstraction of money mediates between human-kind and nature, and always embodies the *deferral* of pleasure, the pleasures of Silenos, and of the satyrs generally, are always direct and immediate. Whereas Midas is an 'ephemeral' mortal, Silenos, like Dionysos, combines animality, humanity, and immortality. It is as if the monetary isolation of the individual (from nature and even from kin) is also isolation from deity. The immortal Silenos, companion of Dionysos, disdains the wealth of even the wealthiest of uninitiated mortals, for wealth – in contrast to mystic happiness – is transient.

How then can we find immortality in a monetised world? A man initiated into the Dionysiac thiasos might thereby become an (immortal) satyr. But that is hardly an option attractive to, say, Plato, who dismisses 'initiations performed by people imitating satyrs and silens' as 'not of the polis' (*Laws* 815). For Plato the philosophical rulers of his ideal polis should have *divine* gold and silver money in their *souls* (*Republic* 416e). In his *Symposium* philosophers are to ascend from corporeal attachments to a vision of something that is abstract, beautiful, and unchanging. This progress is described – by Diotima as reported by Socrates – in terms of the transition from suffering to vision in mystic initiation. It is only through escape from nature, from the corporeal, that immortality is to be obtained.

This new mystic wisdom attempts to reconcile abstraction with immortality, and so is antithetical to the ancient wisdom of Silenus. But we do not have to wait long for some recuperation of the corporeal: Socrates is described as like a satyr, both in his appearance and because his speech – like the music of the satyr Marsyas – possesses its hearers; and he despises wealth (216e1–4). Indeed, philosophy is imagined as sharing in the frenzy of a Dionysiac thiasos (218b3), with the word for sharing (*koinōnein*) implying group solidarity. In the time of Plato it seems that Dionysiac initiation might involve the creation of the unity of the group (Chapter 5) as well as – perhaps – of the individual soul (Chapter 8). With *koinōnein* Plato evokes the corporeal cohesion of the Dionysiac group as an image for the merely intellectual cohesion of philosophers. Six centuries later the Neoplatonist Plotinus uses the same image of Dionysiac frenzy, but only for the unity of the individual philosophical soul (Chapter 8).

Eighteen centuries after Plotinus, individualism has made further progress. We live in a world in which the blinkered power of the men of money not only continues to promote the alienation of individuals from each other and from nature but even threatens to destroy nature itself in global environmental catastrophe. Perhaps that is why the Dionysiac still means something to us, and we can still hear the chorus of Sophokles' *Antigone* when – after the havoc caused by the isolated, money-obsessed tyrant Kreon – they invoke Dionysos to come over the slope of Parnassos or the sounding sea-channel to purify with dance the violent pandemic of the polis (1140–5).

FURTHER READING

Bierl, A. F. (1991), *Dionysos und die griechische Tragödie*. Tübingen: Classica Monacensia 1. An exhaustive account of the mentions of Dionysos in tragedy.

Bruhl, A. (1953), *Liber Pater*. Paris. A comprehensive account of the Roman god who was identified with Dionysos.

Burkert., W. (1987), *Ancient Mystery Cult*. Harvard University Press. The best existing treatment of its theme.

Carpenter, T. H. (1986), *Dionysian Imagery in Archaic Greek Art*. Oxford: Clarendon Press. A cautious and well-illustrated treatment. What survives is almost entirely vase-painting.

Carpenter, T. H. (1997), *Dionysian Imagery in Fifth-Century Athens*. Oxford: Clarendon Press. A cautious and well-illustrated treatment. What survives is almost entirely vase-painting.

Carpenter, T. H. and Faraone, C. A. (1993), *The Masks of Dionysos*. Ithaca and London: Cornell University Press. A collection of essays by various scholars on various aspects of the god, with an excellent bibliography.

Casadio, G. (1999), *Il Vino dell' Anima. Storia del culto di Dioniso a Corinto, Sicione, Trezene*. Rome: Il Calamo. An example of what can be extracted from focusing on a single region of Greece.

Detienne, M. (1979), *Dionysos Slain* (translation of *Dionysos mis à mort*, Paris 1977). Baltimore: Johns Hopkins University Press. Contains a structuralist account of the political significance of the myth of the killing of Dionysos.

Dodds, E. R. (1960), *Euripides Bacchae* (2nd ed.). Oxford University Press. Contains the Greek text and influential Introduction and Commentary.

Henrichs, A. (1978), 'Greek Maenadism from Olympia to Messalina', *Harvard Studies in Classical Philology*. 82.121–60. The best historical account of maenadism, based largely on inscriptions.

Henrichs, A. (1982), 'Changing Dionysiac Identities', in B. F. Meyer and E. P. Sanders (eds), *Self-Definition in the Graeco-Roman World*. London. 137–60, 213–36. Largely on the relation of individual to group in Dionysiac cult.

Henrichs, A. (1984), 'Loss of Self, Suffering, Violence: the Modern View of Dionysus from Nietzsche to Girard', *Harvard Studies in Classical Philology* 88.205–40. A critical overview of modern accounts of Dionysos.

Isler-Kerényi, C. (2001), *Dionysos nella Grecia arcaica*. Pisa and Rome: Istituti Editoriali e Poligrafici Internazionali. An account of Dionysos, and his retinue, in archaic painting that (in contrast to Carpenter) introduces anthropological and historical perspectives.

Jaccottet, A. -F. (2003), *Choisir Dionysos. Les Associations Dionysiaques ou la face cachée du Dionysisme*. Zurich: Akanthus. An indispensable collection and discussion of the numerous inscriptions relating to Dionysiac associations.

Kerényi, C. (1976), *Dionysos. Archetypal Image of Indestructible Life* (translated from the German by R. Mannheim). London: Routledge and Kegan Paul. A Jungian account, with an enormous range of material.

Lada-Richards I. (1999), *Initiating Dionysos*. Oxford University Press. Dionysos as god of mystery-cult is brought to bear on interpreting Aristophanes' *Frogs*.

Lexicon Iconographicum Mythologiae Classicae (1986), vol. 3, 1.414–566, 2.296–456 (plates). A very extensive list of visual images of Dionysos.

McGinty, P. (1978), *Interpretation and Dionysos*. The Hague: Mouton. A lucid account of modern interpretations of Dionysos.

Matz, F. (1968–75), *Die Dionysische Sarkophage*. 4 vols. Berlin. Collects the large number of tombs of the imperial period sculpted with reliefs on Dionysiac themes.

Nietzsche, F. (1872), *Die Geburt der Tragödie aus dem Geist der Musik*. (republished by Reclam, Stuttgart, 1993). Contains a seminal account of the Dionysiac.

Nilsson, M. P. (1957), *The Dionysiac Mysteries of the Hellenistic and Roman Age*. Lund. Somewhat out of date, but one of the very few works of Nilsson to have been translated into English. Other works contain much about Dionysos, for example his two-volume history of Greek religion (*Geschichte der griechischen Religion*).

Otto, W.F. (1965), *Dionysus. Myth and cult* (translated from the German of 1933). Indiana University Press. An ahistorical vision of Dionysos as the embodiment of epiphany and contradiction.

Parker, R. (2005). *Polytheism and Society at Athens*. Oxford University Press. Contains a good recent account of the Dionysiac festivals at Athens.

Rohde, E. (1925) [1894], *Psyche. The Cult of Souls and Belief in Immortality among the Ancient Greeks* (translation from the German (8th edition), reprinted 1987). London: Kegan Paul. Contains an influential account of Dionysiac cult as a cult of souls. Rohde believed that Dionysos arrived in Greece from Thrace, but has now been contradicted by the discovery of Bronze Age texts.

Seaford, R. (1996), *Euripides Bacchae*. Aris and Phillips. Introduction, Greek text, Translation and Commentary. Adduces politics and mystery-cult.

Versnel, H. (1990), *Ter Unis. Isis, Dionysos, Hermes: Three Studies in Henotheism*. Leiden: E. J. Brill. Illuminates Euripides' *Bacchae* from a historical perspective that includes general discussion of the introduction of new gods into Athens.

WORKS CITED

Several of the works in the Further Reading section are cited in the text. Also cited are the following

Bérard, C. (1974), *Anodoi*. Bibliotheca Helvetica Romana 13. Neuchâtel.
Coldiron, M. J. (2004), *Trance and the Transformation of the Actor in Japanese Noh and Balinese Masked Dance-Drama*. Edwin Mellen Press.
Dodds E. R. (1951), *The Greeks and the Irrational*. University of California Press.
Haenchen, E. (1971), *The Acts of the Apostles. A Commentary*. Oxford: Blackwell.
Keuls, E. (1997), *Painter and Poet in Ancient Greece*. Stuttgart: Teubner.
Rouget, G. (1985), *Music and Trance*. Chicago University Press.

INDEX

Related titles from Routledge

Zeus
Ken Dowden

Sovereign ruler of the universe, controller of the weather, all-seeing father of gods and men: Zeus was the chief deity of the ancient Greek pantheon. His places of worship ranged from the household to Olympia, the greatest of all sanctuaries. His significance is reflected in the many chapters dedicated to him in books on Greek religion and myth but this is the first attempt to capture him in the round, in a single volume, for many years.

In a study that is at once masterly and comprehensive, Ken Dowden presents a study of this fascinating god for the new millennium. Myth, cult, art and art are examined, as are philosophy, drama, theology, European painting and much more. Not only is the period of the ancient Greeks covered but that of their predecessors, and above all that of their successors, the Romans. The importance of Zeus in the medieval period and modern times is discussed in a revealing section on reception.

The book contains many and varied illustrations, charts and maps and provides a thorough and accessible, as well as scholarly, introduction to the chief god in the Greek pantheon.

ISBN10: 0–415–30502–0 (hbk)
ISBN10: 0–415–30503–9 (pbk)

ISBN13: 978–0–415–30502–0 (hbk)
ISBN13: 978–0–415–30503–9 (pbk)

Available at all good bookshops
For ordering and further information please visit:
www.routledge.com

Related titles from Routledge

Prometheus
Carol Dougherty

Myths and legends of this rebellious god, who defied Zeus to steal fire for mankind, thrive in art and literature from ancient Greece to the present day. Prometheus' gifts to mortals of the raw materials of culture and technological advancement, along with the curse of despair that followed the enlightenment of humankind, have formed the basis of a poetic and powerful embodiment of the human condition.

Seeking to locate the nature of this compelling tale's continuing relevance throughout history, Carol Dougherty traces a history of the myth from its origins in ancient Greece to its resurgence in the works of the Romantic age and beyond. A Prometheus emerges that was a rebel against Zeus's tyranny to Aeschylus, a defender of political and artistic integrity to Shelley and a symbol of technological innovation during the industrial revolution, his resilience and adaptability illuminating his power and importance in Western culture.

This book provides a comprehensive introduction to the Prometheus myth, emphasising the vitality and flexibility of his myth in a variety of historical, literary, and artistic contexts of the ancient Greeks, the Romantics, and twentieth-century English poet, Tony Harrison. It is an essential introduction to the Promethean myth for readers interested in Classics, the arts and literature alike.

ISBN10: 0–415–32405–X (hbk)
ISBN10: 0–415–32406–8 (pbk)

ISBN13: 978–0–415–32405–X (hbk)
ISBN13: 978–0–415–32406–8 (pbk)

Available at all good bookshops
For ordering and further information please visit:
www.routledge.com

Related titles from Routledge

Medea
Emma Griffiths

Medea, the sorceress of Greek myth and Euripides' vengeful heroine, is famed for the murder of her children after she is banished from her own family and displaced by a new wife. Her reputation as a wronged 'everywoman' of Greek tragedy has helped engender her lasting appeal to the modern age. However, this firmly rooted status has also caused many of the intricacies of her timeless tale to be overlooked.

Emma Griffiths brings into focus previously unexplored themes of the Medea myth, along with providing an incisive introduction to the story and its history. Viewed within its context, the tale reveals fascinating insights into ancient Greece and its ideology, the importance of children, the role of women, and the position of the outsider and barbarian.

The critically sophisticated analysis, expressed in clear and accessible terms, proceeds to examine the persistence of the Medea myth through ancient Rome to the modern day. Placing the myth within a modern context and into analytical frameworks such as psychoanalysis, Griffiths highlights Medea's position in current classical study, as well as her lasting appeal. A vivid portrait of a woman empowered by her exclusion from society, alive with passion and the suffering of wounded love, this book is an indispensable guide to a fascinating mythical figure.

ISBN10: 0–415–30069–X (hbk)
ISBN10: 0–415–30070–3 (hbk)

ISBN13: 978–0–415–30069–X (hbk)
ISBN13: 978–0–415–30070–3 (pbk)

Available at all good bookshops
For ordering and further information please visit:
www.routledge.com